Phonics Games

LEVEL C

Game 1 **Long & Short of It** *Long and Short Vowel Sounds*

Game 2 **Spell It!** *Vowel Digraphs*

Game 3 **Ping Pang Pow!** *Initial Consonant Blends*

Game 4 **Long Vowel Bingo** *Long Vowel Sounds*

Game 5 **What's Up Front?** *Initial Consonant Digraphs*

Game 6 **R-Controlled Bingo** *R-Controlled Vowels*

Game 7 **Syllable Count** *1-, 2-, and 3-Syllable Words*

Correlated to State Standards

EMC 3364

Evan-Moor®
EDUCATIONAL PUBLISHERS
Helping Children Learn since 1979

Editorial Development: Joy Evans
Camille Liscinsky
Jo Ellen Moore
Lisa Vitarisi Mathews
Copy Editing: Carrie Gwynne
Laurie Westrich
Cover/Illustrations: Liliana Potigian/Jo Larsen
Art Direction: Cheryl Puckett
Design/Production: Marcia Smith
Olivia C. Trinidad

Congratulations on your purchase of some of the finest teaching materials in the world.

For information about other Evan-Moor products, call 1-800-777-4362, fax 1-800-777-4332, or visit our Web site, www.evan-moor.com. Entire contents © 2008 EVAN-MOOR CORP. 18 Lower Ragsdale Drive, Monterey, CA 93940-5746. Printed in USA.

How to Use Phonics Games

LEVEL C

Play the games as a follow-up to a phonics lesson, or use a game to target a skill that several students need to practice. The games are also fun "extra-time" or rainy-day recess activities.

Model how to play each type of game, and place the games in an area of your classroom that is easily accessible to students.

Games Include:

Directions

Game boards

Game cards

Answer key

Reproducible activity pages

How to Make a Phonics Game

Steps to Follow:

1. Laminate the directions page, the game boards, the cards, and the answer key(s).

2. Reproduce the activity pages.

3. Place the laminated game supplies and any additional items, such as bean markers or brown paper bags, in a folder that has a closure.

Materials

- laminator
- scissors
- brown paper bags
- game board markers such as beans
- folder that has a closure

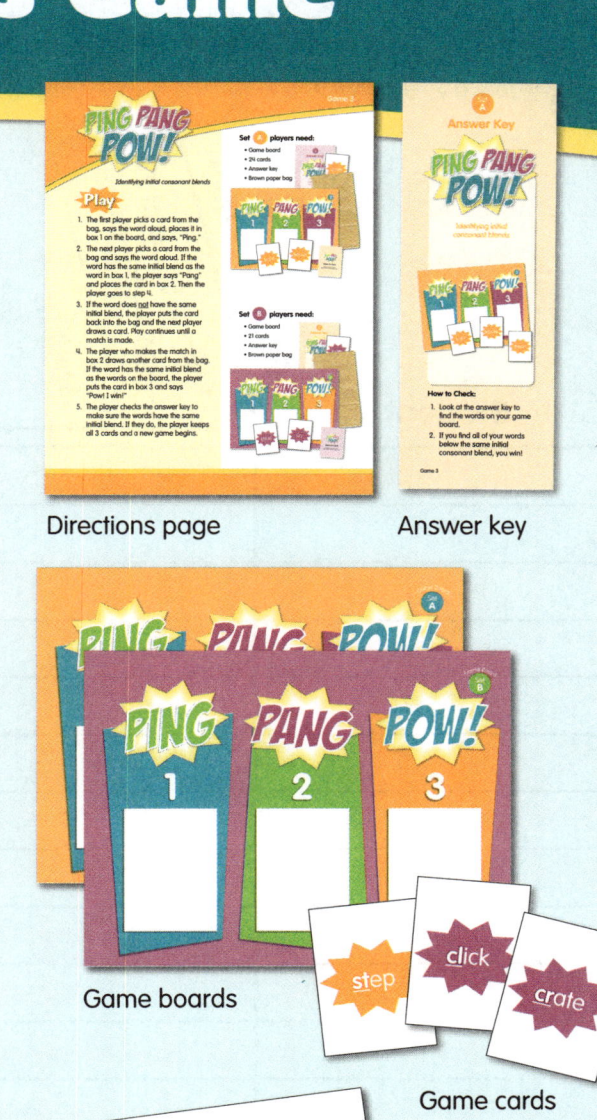

Directions page

Answer key

Game boards

Game cards

Reproducible activity pages

Phonics Games
Checklist

LEVEL C

Student	Games Played	Long & Short of It — Long & Short Vowel Sounds	Spell It! — Vowel Digraphs	Ping Pang Pow! — Initial Consonant Blends	Long Vowel Bingo — Long Vowel Sounds	What's Up Front? — Initial Consonant Digraphs	R-Controlled Bingo — R-Controlled Vowels	Syllable Count — 1-, 2-, & 3-Syllable Words

EMC 3364 • © Evan-Moor Corp.

Long & Short of It

Identifying long and short vowel sounds

Play

1. The first player picks a card out of the bag and reads the word aloud.
2. The player places the card on his or her board in the box that shows the sound that is heard.
3. The next player takes a turn.
4. If the player picks a word that has a sound that is already covered, the card is put back into the bag and the next player takes a turn.

Win

1. The first player to cover all of the boxes on the game board shouts out, "I win!"
2. Players check the answer key to see if the cards are correctly placed.
3. If the player who shouted "I win!" has placed the cards correctly, he or she wins!

Give each player a game board.

Put the cards into a bag.

Answer key

	Short	Long

Game 1

Phonics Games, Level C
EMC 3364 • © Evan-Moor Corp.

Short   Long

 a

 e

i

 o

 u

2

Game 1

Phonics Games, Level C
EMC 3364 • © Evan-Moor Corp.

	Short	**Long**

3

Game 1

Phonics Games, Level C
EMC 3364 • © Evan-Moor Corp.

	Short	Long
 a		
 e		
i		
 o		
 u		

Game 1

Phonics Games, Level C
EMC 3364 • © Evan-Moor Corp.

Short	Long

Game 1

Phonics Games, Level C
EMC 3364 • © Evan-Moor Corp.

	Short	Long

Game 1

Phonics Games, Level C
EMC 3364 • © Evan-Moor Corp.

clap	fan	lamp	past
glass	fact	mess	neck
tent	rest	dent	desk
skip	lick	chin	river
hint	gift	ox	sock
cost	drop	cross	clock
shop	plus	much	club
plug	luck	fun	jump

Game 1

Phonics Games, Level C
EMC 3364 • © Evan-Moor Corp.

Game 1

Phonics Games, Level C
EMC 3364 • © Evan-Moor Corp.

Game 1

Phonics Games, Level C
EMC 3364 • © Evan-Moor Corp.

Game 1

Phonics Games, Level C
EMC 3364 • © Evan-Moor Corp.

Game 1

Phonics Games, Level C
EMC 3364 • © Evan-Moor Corp.

Game 1

Phonics Games, Level C
EMC 3364 • © Evan-Moor Corp.

Game 1

Phonics Games, Level C
EMC 3364 • © Evan-Moor Corp.

Game 1

Phonics Games, Level C
EMC 3364 • © Evan-Moor Corp.

Game 1

Phonics Games, Level C
EMC 3364 • © Evan-Moor Corp.

Game 1

Phonics Games, Level C
EMC 3364 • © Evan-Moor Corp.

Game 1

Phonics Games, Level C
EMC 3364 • © Evan-Moor Corp.

Game 1

Phonics Games, Level C
EMC 3364 • © Evan-Moor Corp.

Game 1

Phonics Games, Level C
EMC 3364 • © Evan-Moor Corp.

Game 1

Phonics Games, Level C
EMC 3364 • © Evan-Moor Corp.

Game 1

Phonics Games, Level C
EMC 3364 • © Evan-Moor Corp.

Game 1

Phonics Games, Level C
EMC 3364 • © Evan-Moor Corp.

Game 1

Phonics Games, Level C
EMC 3364 • © Evan-Moor Corp.

Game 1

Phonics Games, Level C
EMC 3364 • © Evan-Moor Corp.

Game 1

Phonics Games, Level C
EMC 3364 • © Evan-Moor Corp.

Game 1

Phonics Games, Level C
EMC 3364 • © Evan-Moor Corp.

Game 1

Phonics Games, Level C
EMC 3364 • © Evan-Moor Corp.

Game 1

Phonics Games, Level C
EMC 3364 • © Evan-Moor Corp.

Game 1

Phonics Games, Level C
EMC 3364 • © Evan-Moor Corp.

Game 1

Phonics Games, Level C
EMC 3364 • © Evan-Moor Corp.

Game 1

Phonics Games, Level C
EMC 3364 • © Evan-Moor Corp.

Game 1

Phonics Games, Level C
EMC 3364 • © Evan-Moor Corp.

Game 1

Phonics Games, Level C
EMC 3364 • © Evan-Moor Corp.

Game 1

Phonics Games, Level C
EMC 3364 • © Evan-Moor Corp.

Game 1

Phonics Games, Level C
EMC 3364 • © Evan-Moor Corp.

Game 1

Phonics Games, Level C
EMC 3364 • © Evan-Moor Corp.

Game 1

Phonics Games, Level C
EMC 3364 • © Evan-Moor Corp.

Game 1

Phonics Games, Level C
EMC 3364 • © Evan-Moor Corp.

chase	cage	race	skate
snake	tape	page	feet
neat	week	each	beep
seal	dime	pipe	nine
slide	bike	five	tie
globe	rope	rose	hope
bone	whole	mule	tube
blue	tune	huge	flute

Game 1

Phonics Games, Level C
EMC 3364 • © Evan-Moor Corp.

Game 1

Phonics Games, Level C
EMC 3364 • © Evan-Moor Corp.

Game 1

Phonics Games, Level C
EMC 3364 • © Evan-Moor Corp.

Game 1

Phonics Games, Level C
EMC 3364 • © Evan-Moor Corp.

Game 1

Phonics Games, Level C
EMC 3364 • © Evan-Moor Corp.

Game 1

Phonics Games, Level C
EMC 3364 • © Evan-Moor Corp.

Game 1

Phonics Games, Level C
EMC 3364 • © Evan-Moor Corp.

Game 1

Phonics Games, Level C
EMC 3364 • © Evan-Moor Corp.

Game 1

Phonics Games, Level C
EMC 3364 • © Evan-Moor Corp.

Game 1

Phonics Games, Level C
EMC 3364 • © Evan-Moor Corp.

Game 1

Phonics Games, Level C
EMC 3364 • © Evan-Moor Corp.

Game 1

Phonics Games, Level C
EMC 3364 • © Evan-Moor Corp.

Game 1

Phonics Games, Level C
EMC 3364 • © Evan-Moor Corp.

Game 1

Phonics Games, Level C
EMC 3364 • © Evan-Moor Corp.

Game 1

Phonics Games, Level C
EMC 3364 • © Evan-Moor Corp.

Game 1

Phonics Games, Level C
EMC 3364 • © Evan-Moor Corp.

Game 1

Phonics Games, Level C
EMC 3364 • © Evan-Moor Corp.

Game 1

Phonics Games, Level C
EMC 3364 • © Evan-Moor Corp.

Game 1

Phonics Games, Level C
EMC 3364 • © Evan-Moor Corp.

Game 1

Phonics Games, Level C
EMC 3364 • © Evan-Moor Corp.

Game 1

Phonics Games, Level C
EMC 3364 • © Evan-Moor Corp.

Game 1

Phonics Games, Level C
EMC 3364 • © Evan-Moor Corp.

Game 1

Phonics Games, Level C
EMC 3364 • © Evan-Moor Corp.

Game 1

Phonics Games, Level C
EMC 3364 • © Evan-Moor Corp.

Game 1

Phonics Games, Level C
EMC 3364 • © Evan-Moor Corp.

Game 1

Phonics Games, Level C
EMC 3364 • © Evan-Moor Corp.

Game 1

Phonics Games, Level C
EMC 3364 • © Evan-Moor Corp.

Game 1

Phonics Games, Level C
EMC 3364 • © Evan-Moor Corp.

Game 1

Phonics Games, Level C
EMC 3364 • © Evan-Moor Corp.

Game 1

Phonics Games, Level C
EMC 3364 • © Evan-Moor Corp.

Game 1

Phonics Games, Level C
EMC 3364 • © Evan-Moor Corp.

Game 1

Phonics Games, Level C
EMC 3364 • © Evan-Moor Corp.

Answer Key

Long & Short of It

Identifying long and short vowel sounds

How to Check:

1. Look at the word card in the **short *a*** box on your game board.

2. See if the word matches one of the words in the list below **short *a*** on the answer key.

3. Use the answer key to check your other word cards.

a

Short a		Long a	
clap	glass	cage	skate
fact	lamp	chase	snake
fan	past	page	tape
		race	

e

Short e		Long e	
dent	neck	beep	neat
desk	rest	each	seal
mess	tent	feet	week

i

Short i		Long i	
chin	lick	bike	pipe
gift	river	dime	slide
hint	skip	five	tie
		nine	

fold

o

Short o		Long o	
clock	ox	bone	rope
cost	shop	globe	rose
cross	sock	hope	whole
drop			

u

Short u		Long u	
club	much	blue	mule
fun	plug	flute	tube
jump	plus	huge	tune
luck			

Name _____

What's That Sound?

Say each word. Draw a line to show what vowel sound you hear.

short		long	
blend •	• a	chase •	• a
boss •	• e	huge •	• e
clap •	• i	sleep •	• i
jump •	• o	bone •	• o
fin •	• u	fine •	• u

Color the Blanket

Read each word.
Color the square to match the short (◡) or long (—) vowel sound you hear.

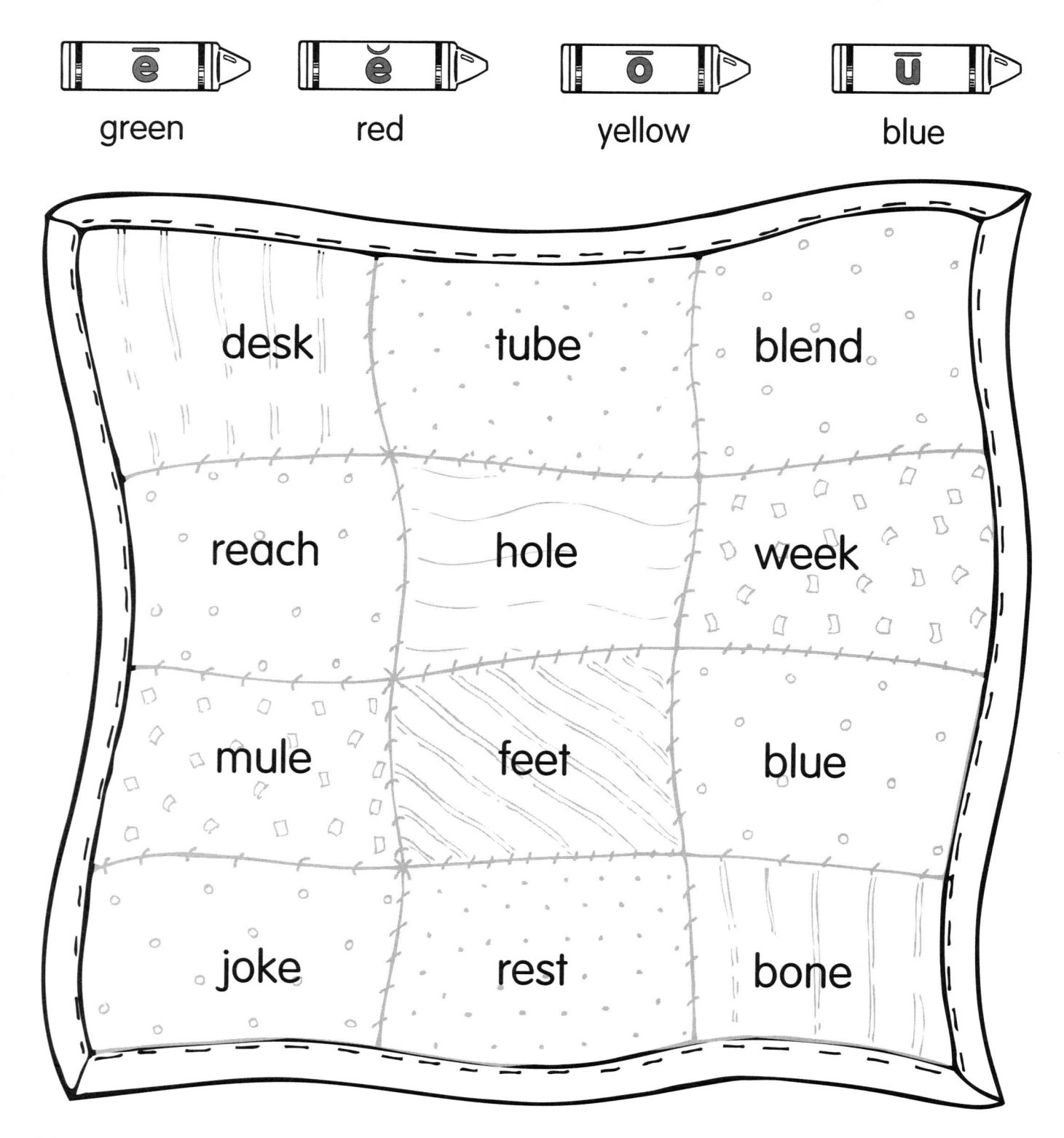

green   red   yellow   blue

desk	tube	blend
reach	hole	week
mule	feet	blue
joke	rest	bone

Spell It!

Spelling words with vowel digraphs

Play

1. Players look at the pictures on their game boards and think about which letters they need to spell each picture name.

2. The first player picks a letter card out of the bag. If the player needs the letters to spell a word, he or she places the letter card in the correct box on his or her board and takes another turn.

3. If the player does <u>not</u> need the letters, he or she puts the card back into the bag and the next player takes a turn.

Win

1. The first player to spell all three words shouts out, "Spell it!"

2. Players check the answer key to see if the words are spelled correctly.

3. If the player who shouted "Spell it!" spelled all three words correctly, he or she wins!

Give each player a game board.

Put the cards into a bag.

Answer key

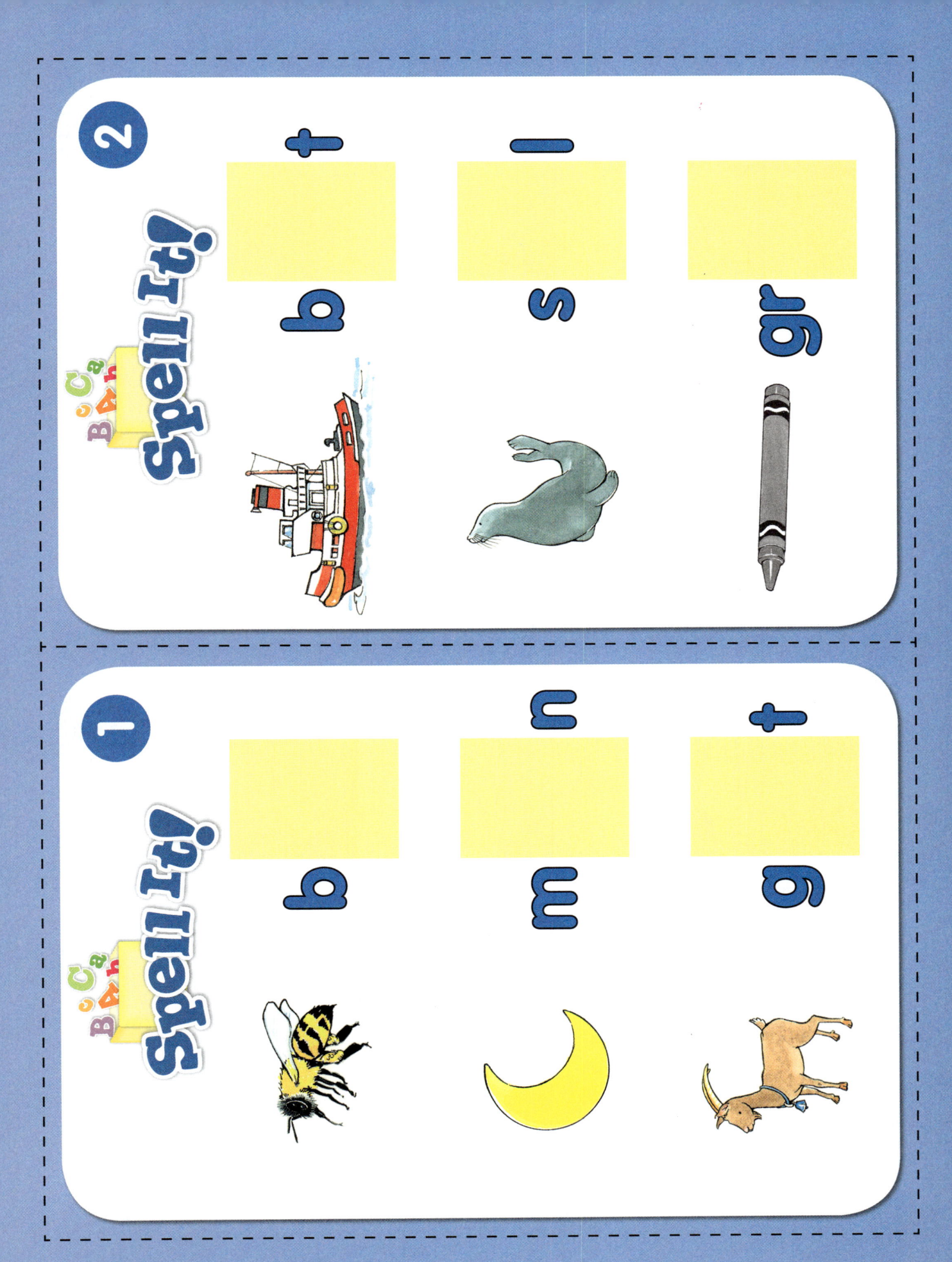

Game 2

Phonics Games, Level C
EMC 3364 • © Evan-Moor Corp.

Game 2

Phonics Games, Level C
EMC 3364 • © Evan-Moor Corp.

Spell it!

4

p [____] br

p [____] j

t [____] l

Spell it!

3

p [____] b

f [____] l

u [____] sp

Game 2

Phonics Games, Level C
EMC 3364 • © Evan-Moor Corp.

Game 2

Phonics Games, Level C
EMC 3364 • © Evan-Moor Corp.

6 Spell It!

d [____] r

b [____] t

gl [____]

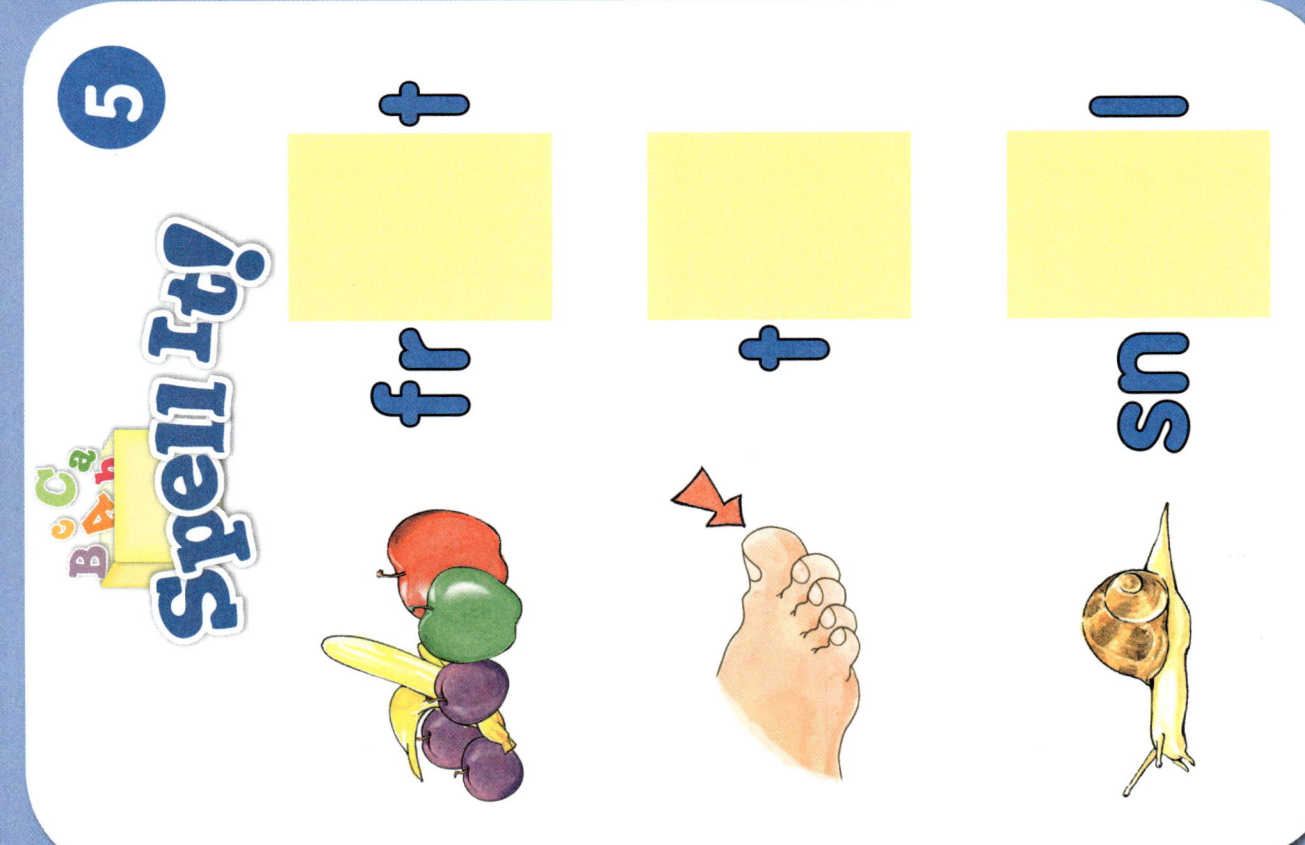

5 Spell It!

fr [____] t

f [____] t

sn [____] l

Spell It!

Game 2

Phonics Games, Level C
EMC 3364 • © Evan-Moor Corp.

Spell It!

Game 2

Phonics Games, Level C
EMC 3364 • © Evan-Moor Corp.

Spell It!
Game 2
Phonics Games, Level C
EMC 3364

Spell It!
Game 2
Phonics Games, Level C
EMC 3364
© Evan-Moor Corp.

Spell It!
Game 2
Phonics Games, Level C
EMC 3364
© Evan-Moor Corp.

Spell It!
Game 2
Phonics Games, Level C
EMC 3364
© Evan-Moor Corp.

Spell It!
Game 2
Phonics Games, Level C
EMC 3364
© Evan-Moor Corp.

Spell It!
Game 2
Phonics Games, Level C
EMC 3364
© Evan-Moor Corp.

Spell It!
Game 2
Phonics Games, Level C
EMC 3364
© Evan-Moor Corp.

Spell It!
Game 2
Phonics Games, Level C
EMC 3364
© Evan-Moor Corp.

Spell It!
Game 2
Phonics Games, Level C
EMC 3364
© Evan-Moor Corp.

Spell It!
Game 2
Phonics Games, Level C
EMC 3364
© Evan-Moor Corp.

Spell It!
Game 2
Phonics Games, Level C
EMC 3364
© Evan-Moor Corp.

Spell It!
Game 2
Phonics Games, Level C
EMC 3364
© Evan-Moor Corp.

Spell It!
Game 2
Phonics Games, Level C
EMC 3364
© Evan-Moor Corp.

Spell It!
Game 2
Phonics Games, Level C
EMC 3364
© Evan-Moor Corp.

Spell It!
Game 2
Phonics Games, Level C
EMC 3364
© Evan-Moor Corp.

Spell It!
Game 2
Phonics Games, Level C
EMC 3364
© Evan-Moor Corp.

Spell It!
Game 2
Phonics Games, Level C
EMC 3364
© Evan-Moor Corp.

Spell It!
Game 2
Phonics Games, Level C
EMC 3364
© Evan-Moor Corp.

Spell It!
Game 2
Phonics Games, Level C
EMC 3364
© Evan-Moor Corp.

Spell It!
Game 2
Phonics Games, Level C
EMC 3364
© Evan-Moor Corp.

Spell It!
Game 2
Phonics Games, Level C
EMC 3364
© Evan-Moor Corp.

Spell It!
Game 2
Phonics Games, Level C
EMC 3364
© Evan-Moor Corp.

Spell It!
Game 2
Phonics Games, Level C
EMC 3364
© Evan-Moor Corp.

Spell It!
Game 2
Phonics Games, Level C
EMC 3364
© Evan-Moor Corp.

Spell It!
Game 2
Phonics Games, Level C
EMC 3364
© Evan-Moor Corp.

Spell It!
Game 2
Phonics Games, Level C
EMC 3364
© Evan-Moor Corp.

Spell It!
Game 2
Phonics Games, Level C
EMC 3364
© Evan-Moor Corp.

Spell It!
Game 2
Phonics Games, Level C
EMC 3364
© Evan-Moor Corp.

Spell It!
Game 2
Phonics Games, Level C
EMC 3364
© Evan-Moor Corp.

Spell It!
Game 2
Phonics Games, Level C
EMC 3364
© Evan-Moor Corp.

Spell It!
Game 2
Phonics Games, Level C
EMC 3364
© Evan-Moor Corp.

Spell It!
Game 2
Phonics Games, Level C
EMC 3364
© Evan-Moor Corp.

Spell It!
Game 2
Phonics Games, Level C
EMC 3364
© Evan-Moor Corp.

Spell It!
Game 2
Phonics Games, Level C
EMC 3364
© Evan-Moor Corp.

Spell It!
Game 2
Phonics Games, Level C
EMC 3364
© Evan-Moor Corp.

Spell It!
Game 2
Phonics Games, Level C
EMC 3364
© Evan-Moor Corp.

Spell It!
Game 2
Phonics Games, Level C
EMC 3364
© Evan-Moor Corp.

Spell It!
Game 2
Phonics Games, Level C
EMC 3364
© Evan-Moor Corp.

Spell It!
Game 2
Phonics Games, Level C
EMC 3364
© Evan-Moor Corp.

Spell It!
Game 2
Phonics Games, Level C
EMC 3364
© Evan-Moor Corp.

Spell It!
Game 2
Phonics Games, Level C
EMC 3364
© Evan-Moor Corp.

Spell It!
Game 2
Phonics Games, Level C
EMC 3364
© Evan-Moor Corp.

Spell It!
Game 2
Phonics Games, Level C
EMC 3364
© Evan-Moor Corp.

Spell It!
Game 2
Phonics Games, Level C
EMC 3364
© Evan-Moor Corp.

Spell It!
Game 2
Phonics Games, Level C
EMC 3364
© Evan-Moor Corp.

Spell It!
Game 2
Phonics Games, Level C
EMC 3364
© Evan-Moor Corp.

Spell It!
Game 2
Phonics Games, Level C
EMC 3364
© Evan-Moor Corp.

Spell It!
Game 2
Phonics Games, Level C
EMC 3364
© Evan-Moor Corp.

Spell It!

Spelling words with vowel digraphs

How to Check:

1. Find the picture of your game board.
2. Check to see if you spelled the words correctly.

Spell It! 1

b | ee

m | oo | n

g | oa | t

Spell It! 2

b | oa | t

s | ea | l

gr | ay

Spell It! 3

b | ow

l | ea | f

sp | oo | n

Spell It! 4

br | ai | d

j | ee | p

l | igh | t

Spell It! 5

fr | ui | t

t | oe

sn | ai | l

Spell It! 6

d | ee | r

b | oo | t

gl | ue

fold

Sorting Sounds

Say each word. Listen to the vowel sound.
Write the word below the vowel sound you hear.

bite	deal	glue	moan	pail	tool
crow	fruit	jeep	night	spool	tray

long a	**long e**	**long i**

long o	**long u**

Vowel Digraphs

Say each picture name.
Write the missing letters to spell the word.

| oo | oa | ea | ui | ee | igh | ue |

1.

m __ __ n

2.

l __ __ t

3.

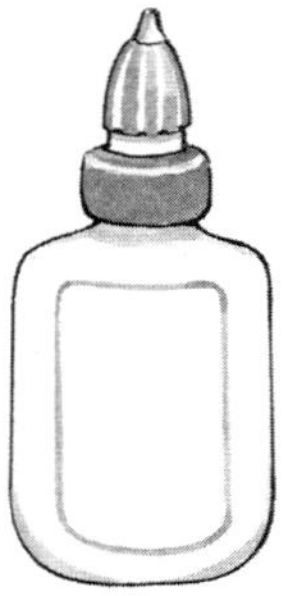

gl __ __

4.

g __ __ t

5.

l __ __ f

6.

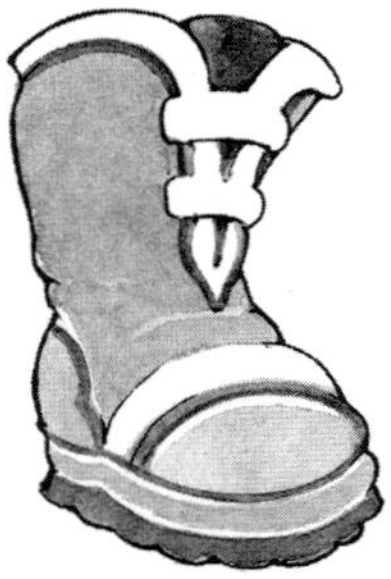

b __ __ t

7.

s __ __ l

8.

b __ __

9.

fr __ __ t

PING PANG POW!

Identifying initial consonant blends

Play

1. The first player picks a card from the bag, says the word aloud, places it in box 1 on the board, and says, "Ping."

2. The next player picks a card from the bag and says the word aloud. If the word has the same initial blend as the word in box 1, the player says, "Pang" and places the card in box 2. Then the player goes to step 4.

3. If the word does <u>not</u> have the same initial blend, the player puts the card back into the bag and the next player draws a card. Play continues until a match is made.

4. The player who makes the match in box 2 draws another card from the bag. If the word has the same initial blend as the words on the board, the player puts the card in box 3 and says, "Pow! I win!"

5. The player checks the answer key to make sure the words have the same initial blend. If they do, the player keeps all 3 cards and a new game begins.

Set A players need:

- Game board
- 24 cards
- Answer key
- Brown paper bag

Set B players need:

- Game board
- 21 cards
- Answer key
- Brown paper bag

POW!

3

PANG

2

PING

1

Game 3

Phonics Games, Level C
EMC 3364 • © Evan-Moor Corp.

POW!

3

PANG

2

PING

1

Game 3

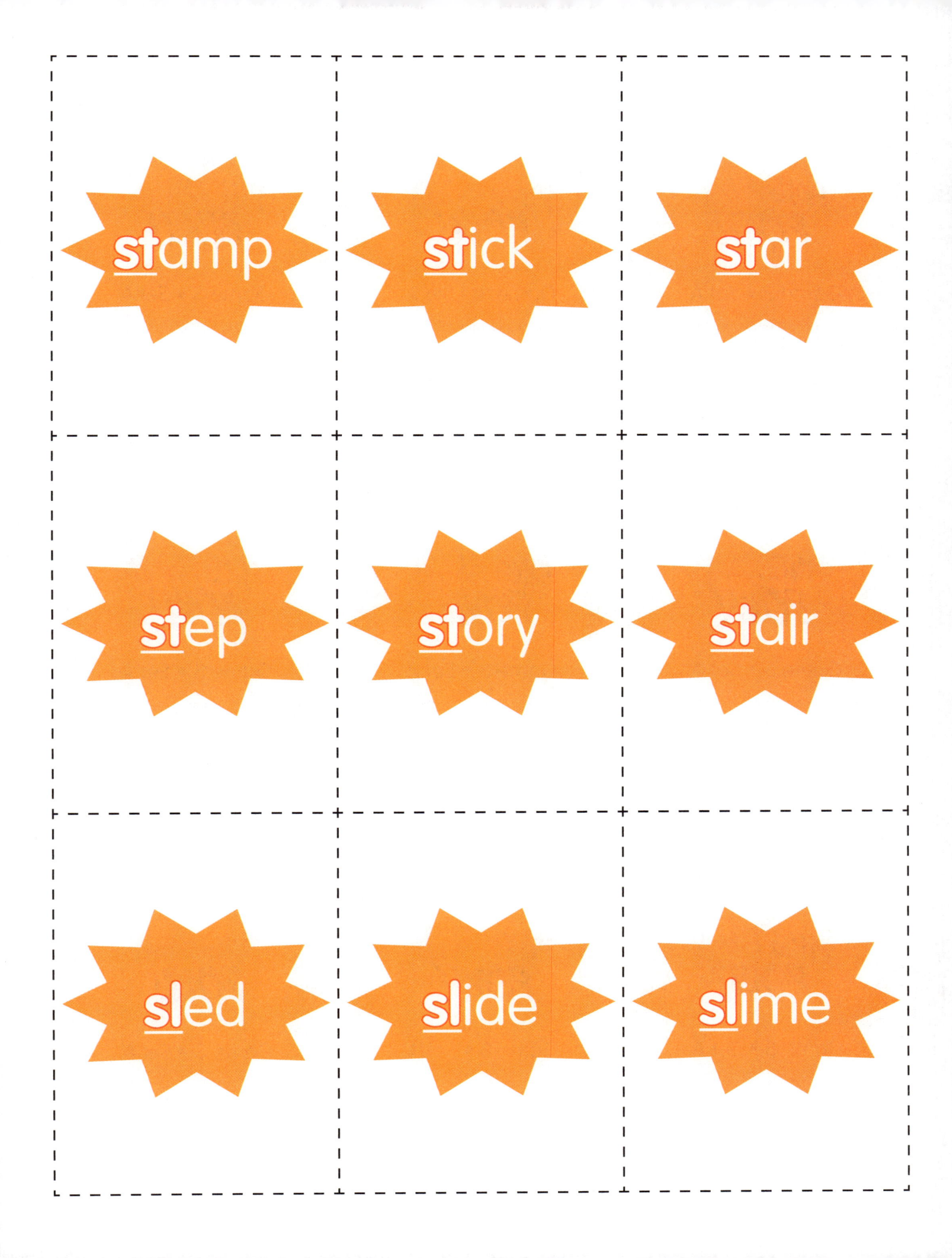

Game 3 • Set A

Phonics Games, Level C
EMC 3364 • © Evan-Moor Corp.

Game 3 • Set A

Phonics Games, Level C
EMC 3364 • © Evan-Moor Corp.

Game 3 • Set A

Phonics Games, Level C
EMC 3364 • © Evan-Moor Corp.

Game 3 • Set A

Phonics Games, Level C
EMC 3364 • © Evan-Moor Corp.

Game 3 • Set A

Phonics Games, Level C
EMC 3364 • © Evan-Moor Corp.

Game 3 • Set A

Phonics Games, Level C
EMC 3364 • © Evan-Moor Corp.

Game 3 • Set A

Phonics Games, Level C
EMC 3364 • © Evan-Moor Corp.

Game 3 • Set A

Phonics Games, Level C
EMC 3364 • © Evan-Moor Corp.

Game 3 • Set A

Phonics Games, Level C
EMC 3364 • © Evan-Moor Corp.

Game 3 • Set A

Phonics Games, Level C
EMC 3364 • © Evan-Moor Corp.

Game 3 • Set A

Phonics Games, Level C
EMC 3364 • © Evan-Moor Corp.

Game 3 • Set A

Phonics Games, Level C
EMC 3364 • © Evan-Moor Corp.

Game 3 • Set A

Phonics Games, Level C
EMC 3364 • © Evan-Moor Corp.

Game 3 • Set A

Phonics Games, Level C
EMC 3364 • © Evan-Moor Corp.

Game 3 • Set A

Phonics Games, Level C
EMC 3364 • © Evan-Moor Corp.

Game 3 • Set A

Phonics Games, Level C
EMC 3364 • © Evan-Moor Corp.

Game 3 • Set A

Phonics Games, Level C
EMC 3364 • © Evan-Moor Corp.

Game 3 • Set A

Phonics Games, Level C
EMC 3364 • © Evan-Moor Corp.

Game 3 • Set A

Phonics Games, Level C
EMC 3364 • © Evan-Moor Corp.

Game 3 • Set A

Phonics Games, Level C
EMC 3364 • © Evan-Moor Corp.

Game 3 • Set A

Phonics Games, Level C
EMC 3364 • © Evan-Moor Corp.

Game 3 • Set A

Phonics Games, Level C
EMC 3364 • © Evan-Moor Corp.

Game 3 • Set A

Phonics Games, Level C
EMC 3364 • © Evan-Moor Corp.

Game 3 • Set A

Phonics Games, Level C
EMC 3364 • © Evan-Moor Corp.

Game 3 • Set B

Phonics Games, Level C
EMC 3364 • © Evan-Moor Corp.

Game 3 • Set B

Phonics Games, Level C
EMC 3364 • © Evan-Moor Corp.

Game 3 • Set B

Phonics Games, Level C
EMC 3364 • © Evan-Moor Corp.

Game 3 • Set B

Phonics Games, Level C
EMC 3364 • © Evan-Moor Corp.

Game 3 • Set B

Phonics Games, Level C
EMC 3364 • © Evan-Moor Corp.

Game 3 • Set B

Phonics Games, Level C
EMC 3364 • © Evan-Moor Corp.

Game 3 • Set B

Phonics Games, Level C
EMC 3364 • © Evan-Moor Corp.

Game 3 • Set B

Phonics Games, Level C
EMC 3364 • © Evan-Moor Corp.

Game 3 • Set B

Phonics Games, Level C
EMC 3364 • © Evan-Moor Corp.

Game 3 • Set B

Phonics Games, Level C
EMC 3364 • © Evan-Moor Corp.

Game 3 • Set B

Phonics Games, Level C
EMC 3364 • © Evan-Moor Corp.

Game 3 • Set B

Phonics Games, Level C
EMC 3364 • © Evan-Moor Corp.

Game 3 • Set B

Phonics Games, Level C
EMC 3364 • © Evan-Moor Corp.

Game 3 • Set B

Phonics Games, Level C
EMC 3364 • © Evan-Moor Corp.

Game 3 • Set B

Phonics Games, Level C
EMC 3364 • © Evan-Moor Corp.

Game 3 • Set B

Phonics Games, Level C
EMC 3364 • © Evan-Moor Corp.

Game 3 • Set B

Phonics Games, Level C
EMC 3364 • © Evan-Moor Corp.

Game 3 • Set B

Phonics Games, Level C
EMC 3364 • © Evan-Moor Corp.

Game 3 • Set B

Phonics Games, Level C
EMC 3364 • © Evan-Moor Corp.

Game 3 • Set B

Phonics Games, Level C
EMC 3364 • © Evan-Moor Corp.

Game 3 • Set B

Phonics Games, Level C
EMC 3364 • © Evan-Moor Corp.

Identifying initial consonant blends

How to Check:

1. Look at the answer key to find the words on your game board.

2. If you find all of your words below the same initial consonant blend, you win!

Identifying initial consonant blends

How to Check:

1. Look at the answer key to find the words on your game board.

2. If you find all of your words below the same initial consonant blend, you win!

cl-

clap	clay	clear
click	clock	close

cr-

crab	crate	cream
cross	crow	cry

fr-

frame	free	fry

pl-

plan	plant	plate
plot	plug	plus

br-

brass	brave	bread
brick	broke	brother

sl-

slam	slap	sled
slide	slime	slow

sm-

small	smart	smash
smell	smile	smoke

st-

stair	stamp	star
step	stick	story

Name _____

It Begins With...

Each picture word is missing its beginning letters.
Write the letters that complete each word.

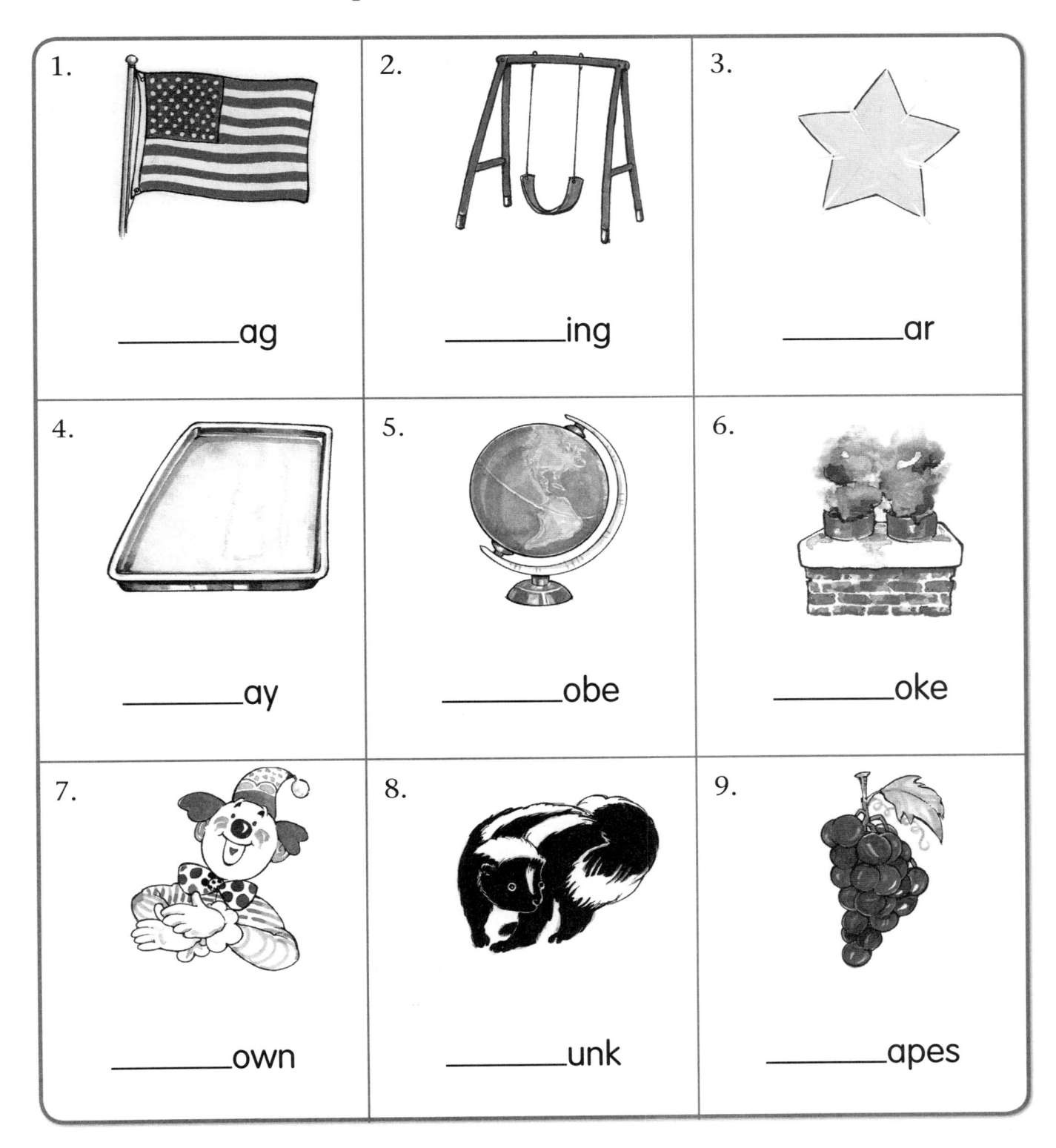

1. _____ag

2. _____ing

3. _____ar

4. _____ay

5. _____obe

6. _____oke

7. _____own

8. _____unk

9. _____apes

Hear the Blend

Say each picture name.
Fill in the circle next to the blend you hear at the beginning of the word.

1. ○ br ● cr ○ gr	**2.** ○ sl ○ gl ○ pl
3. ○ pl ○ sl ○ fl	**4.** ○ br ○ pr ○ gr
5. ○ gr ○ cr ○ tr	**6.** ○ gl ○ fl ○ bl
7. ○ sm ○ sp ○ sn	**8.** ○ sm ○ sl ○ st

Long Vowel BINGO

Identifying words with long vowel sounds

Play

1. Place the large vowel cards faceup in a row in front of the caller.

2. The caller picks a word card from the bag. The caller says the word aloud and does not show the card.

3. The players look for the word on their game boards. If they find the word, they cover it with a marker.

4. The caller places the word card below the correct vowel card and picks another word card from the bag.

Win

1. A player must cover a row of words to win. The row can go up and down, across, or diagonally.

2. The first player to cover a row calls out, "Bingo!"

3. The player reads the words aloud. The caller checks to make sure all of the words are below the vowel cards. If they are, the player wins!

Each player needs:
- 1 game board
- Markers (such as beans)

The caller needs:
- Vowel cards
- Word cards

Put the word cards into a bag.

Long Vowel BINGO 1

cape	three	kite	boat	fruit
toe	light	gray	night	tea
plate	she	FREE	dime	pie
crow	bead	tie	street	pool
chain	fine	bean	high	coach

Game 4

Phonics Games, Level C
EMC 3364 • © Evan-Moor Corp.

Long Vowel BINGO 2

nine	coat	suit	tea	cane
doe	paint	hay	sleep	go
bead	fruit	FREE	plate	high
peas	snow	bee	kite	she
pie	clean	three	cage	pail

Game 4

Phonics Games, Level C
EMC 3364 • © Evan-Moor Corp.

Long Vowel BINGO 3

goat	light	chain	school	fine
due	tie	peas	night	coat
glue	so	FREE	cane	clean
bead	dime	toe	juice	tooth
nine	cape	sleep	day	crow

Game 4

Phonics Games, Level C
EMC 3364 • © Evan-Moor Corp.

Long Vowel BINGO 4

blue	snow	cage	high	street
paint	suit	hay	tea	pool
bee	chain	FREE	day	doe
boat	gray	so	nine	school
go	bean	coach	glue	she

Game 4

Phonics Games, Level C
EMC 3364 • © Evan-Moor Corp.

light	clean	tie	goat	hay
snow	plate	glue	dime	so
due	tea	FREE	pool	three
cage	pie	day	she	night
fruit	kite	fine	gray	bee

Game 4

Phonics Games, Level C
EMC 3364 • © Evan-Moor Corp.

Long Vowel BINGO 6

peas	coat	sleep	crow	suit
doe	boat	chain	fine	bean
fruit	day	FREE	go	pail
coach	blue	toe	cane	due
juice	high	goat	tooth	tea

Game 4

Phonics Games, Level C
EMC 3364 • © Evan-Moor Corp.

a cape	**a** gray	**a** pail	**a** cage
a plate	**a** chain	**a** hay	**a** paint
a cane	**a** day	**e** bee	**e** three
e bean	**e** clean	**e** tea	**e** sleep
e peas	**e** she	**e** street	**e** bead
i kite	**i** nine	**i** tie	**i** night

Game 4

Phonics Games, Level C
EMC 3364
© Evan-Moor Corp.

Game 4

Phonics Games, Level C
EMC 3364
© Evan-Moor Corp.

Game 4

Phonics Games, Level C
EMC 3364
© Evan-Moor Corp.

Game 4

Phonics Games, Level C
EMC 3364
© Evan-Moor Corp.

Game 4

Phonics Games, Level C
EMC 3364
© Evan-Moor Corp.

Game 4

Phonics Games, Level C
EMC 3364
© Evan-Moor Corp.

Game 4

Phonics Games, Level C
EMC 3364
© Evan-Moor Corp.

Game 4

Phonics Games, Level C
EMC 3364
© Evan-Moor Corp.

Game 4

Phonics Games, Level C
EMC 3364
© Evan-Moor Corp.

Game 4

Phonics Games, Level C
EMC 3364
© Evan-Moor Corp.

Game 4

Phonics Games, Level C
EMC 3364
© Evan-Moor Corp.

Game 4

Phonics Games, Level C
EMC 3364
© Evan-Moor Corp.

Game 4

Phonics Games, Level C
EMC 3364
© Evan-Moor Corp.

Game 4

Phonics Games, Level C
EMC 3364
© Evan-Moor Corp.

Game 4

Phonics Games, Level C
EMC 3364
© Evan-Moor Corp.

Game 4

Phonics Games, Level C
EMC 3364
© Evan-Moor Corp.

Game 4

Phonics Games, Level C
EMC 3364
© Evan-Moor Corp.

Game 4

Phonics Games, Level C
EMC 3364
© Evan-Moor Corp.

Game 4

Phonics Games, Level C
EMC 3364
© Evan-Moor Corp.

Game 4

Phonics Games, Level C
EMC 3364
© Evan-Moor Corp.

Game 4

Phonics Games, Level C
EMC 3364
© Evan-Moor Corp.

Game 4

Phonics Games, Level C
EMC 3364
© Evan-Moor Corp.

Game 4

Phonics Games, Level C
EMC 3364
© Evan-Moor Corp.

Game 4

Phonics Games, Level C
EMC 3364
© Evan-Moor Corp.

i pie	**i** high	**i** light	**i** dime
i fine	**o** boat	**o** coat	**o** goat
o toe	**o** so	**o** doe	**o** snow
o go	**o** crow	**o** coach	**u** fruit
u suit	**u** glue	**u** blue	**u** juice
u tooth	**u** pool	**u** school	**u** due

Game 4

Phonics Games, Level C
EMC 3364
© Evan-Moor Corp.

Game 4

Phonics Games, Level C
EMC 3364
© Evan-Moor Corp.

Game 4

Phonics Games, Level C
EMC 3364
© Evan-Moor Corp.

Game 4

Phonics Games, Level C
EMC 3364
© Evan-Moor Corp.

Game 4

Phonics Games, Level C
EMC 3364
© Evan-Moor Corp.

Game 4

Phonics Games, Level C
EMC 3364
© Evan-Moor Corp.

Game 4

Phonics Games, Level C
EMC 3364
© Evan-Moor Corp.

Game 4

Phonics Games, Level C
EMC 3364
© Evan-Moor Corp.

Game 4

Phonics Games, Level C
EMC 3364
© Evan-Moor Corp.

Game 4

Phonics Games, Level C
EMC 3364
© Evan-Moor Corp.

Game 4

Phonics Games, Level C
EMC 3364
© Evan-Moor Corp.

Game 4

Phonics Games, Level C
EMC 3364
© Evan-Moor Corp.

Game 4

Phonics Games, Level C
EMC 3364
© Evan-Moor Corp.

Game 4

Phonics Games, Level C
EMC 3364
© Evan-Moor Corp.

Game 4

Phonics Games, Level C
EMC 3364
© Evan-Moor Corp.

Game 4

Phonics Games, Level C
EMC 3364
© Evan-Moor Corp.

Game 4

Phonics Games, Level C
EMC 3364
© Evan-Moor Corp.

Game 4

Phonics Games, Level C
EMC 3364
© Evan-Moor Corp.

Game 4

Phonics Games, Level C
EMC 3364
© Evan-Moor Corp.

Game 4

Phonics Games, Level C
EMC 3364
© Evan-Moor Corp.

Game 4

Phonics Games, Level C
EMC 3364
© Evan-Moor Corp.

Game 4

Phonics Games, Level C
EMC 3364
© Evan-Moor Corp.

Game 4

Phonics Games, Level C
EMC 3364
© Evan-Moor Corp.

Game 4

Phonics Games, Level C
EMC 3364
© Evan-Moor Corp.

a

e

i

o

u

Game 4

Phonics Games, Level C
EMC 3364 • © Evan-Moor Corp.

Game 4

Phonics Games, Level C
EMC 3364 • © Evan-Moor Corp.

Game 4

Phonics Games, Level C
EMC 3364 • © Evan-Moor Corp.

Game 4

Phonics Games, Level C
EMC 3364 • © Evan-Moor Corp.

Game 4

Phonics Games, Level C
EMC 3364 • © Evan-Moor Corp.

Long Vowel Sounds

1. Circle the letters in each word that make the **long _a_** sound.

   rail   stay   page

2. Circle the letters in each word that make the **long _u_** sound.

   pool   glue   juice

3. Circle the letters in each word that make the **long _i_** sound.

   bike   might   pies

4. Circle the letters in each word that make the **long _o_** sound.

   know   vote   goat

5. Circle the letters in each word that make the **long _e_** sound.

   clean   teeth   we

About Moose

Read about moose. Look at the underlined words.
Write the words in the chart to show what long vowel sounds you hear.

1. <u>Moose</u> are large animals.

2. They live in forests and near <u>lakes</u>.

3. They <u>like</u> to <u>wade</u> in the <u>blue</u> water.

4. They <u>eat</u> the plants that <u>grow</u> there.

5. Moose are <u>very</u> tall.

6. They can eat twigs that are <u>high</u> on <u>trees</u>.

7. They also can walk in <u>deep</u> <u>snow</u>.

a	e	i	o	u

Spelling words with initial consonant digraphs

Play

1. The first player picks a card from the bag, reads it aloud, and places it in the box next to the picture and the word it completes. Then the player reads the word aloud.

2. If the card does <u>not</u> complete a word on the player's game board, the player puts the card back into the bag and the next player takes a turn.

Win

1. The first player to complete all six words shouts out, "I win!"

2. Players check the answer key to see if the cards have been placed next to the correct pictures and incomplete words.

3. If the player who shouted "I win!" has correctly placed the cards, he or she wins!

Give each player a game board.

Put the cards into a bag.

Answer key

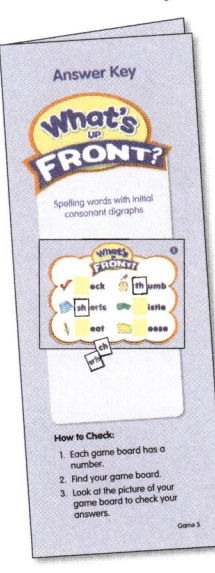

What's Up Front? • Game 5

Phonics Games, Level C • EMC 3364 • © Evan-Moor Corp.

What's UP FRONT?

irty

ell

eck

30

ain

eat

irt

Game 5

Phonics Games, Level C
EMC 3364 • © Evan-Moor Corp.

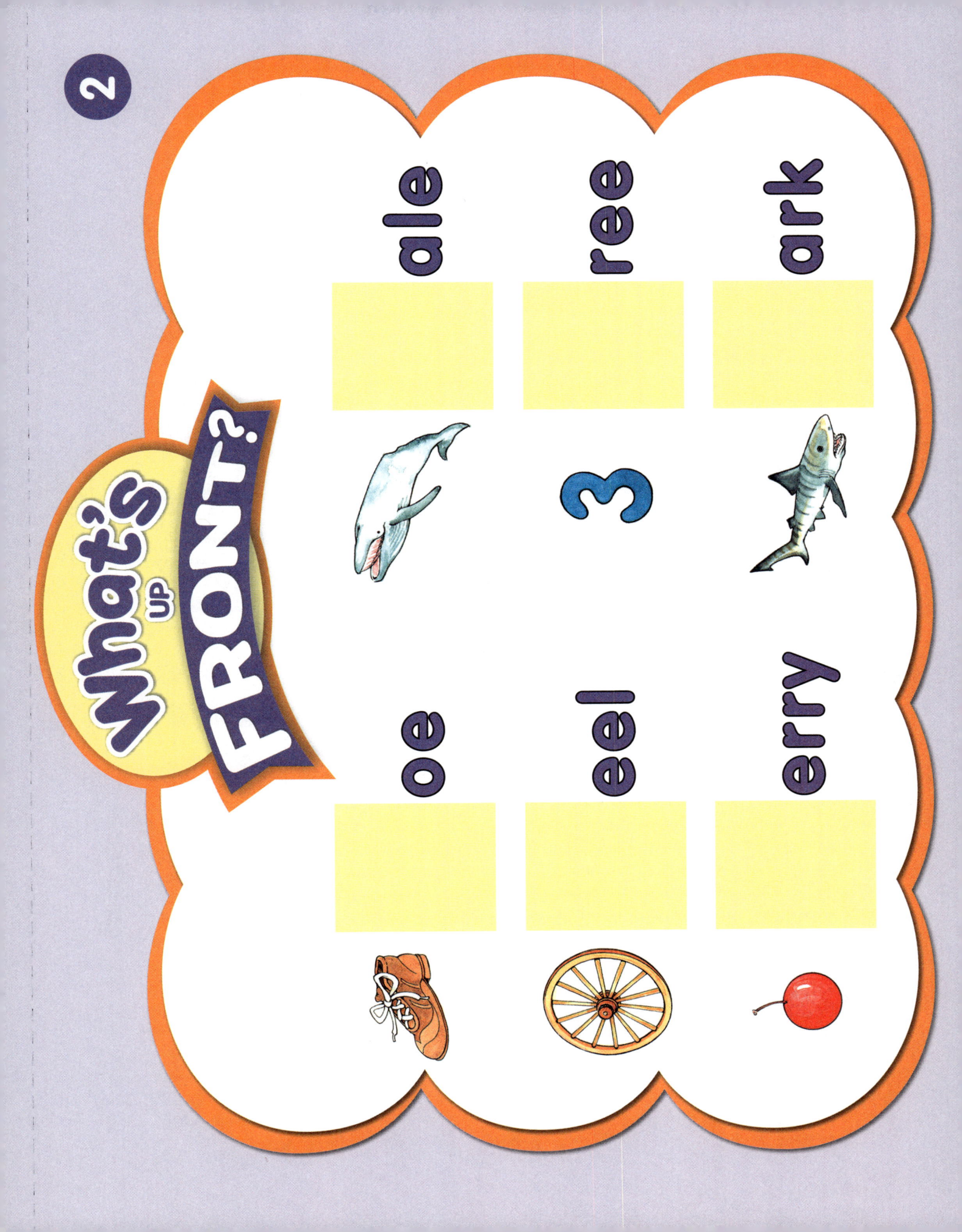

Game 5

3

What's UP FRONT?

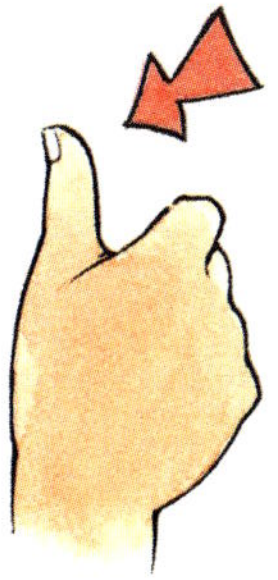

umb

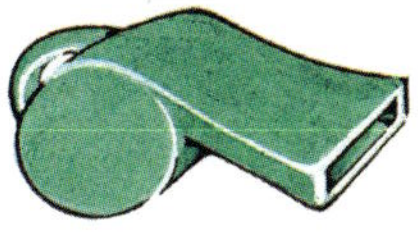

istle

eese

eck

orts

eat

Game 5

Phonics Games, Level C
EMC 3364 • © Evan-Moor Corp.

4

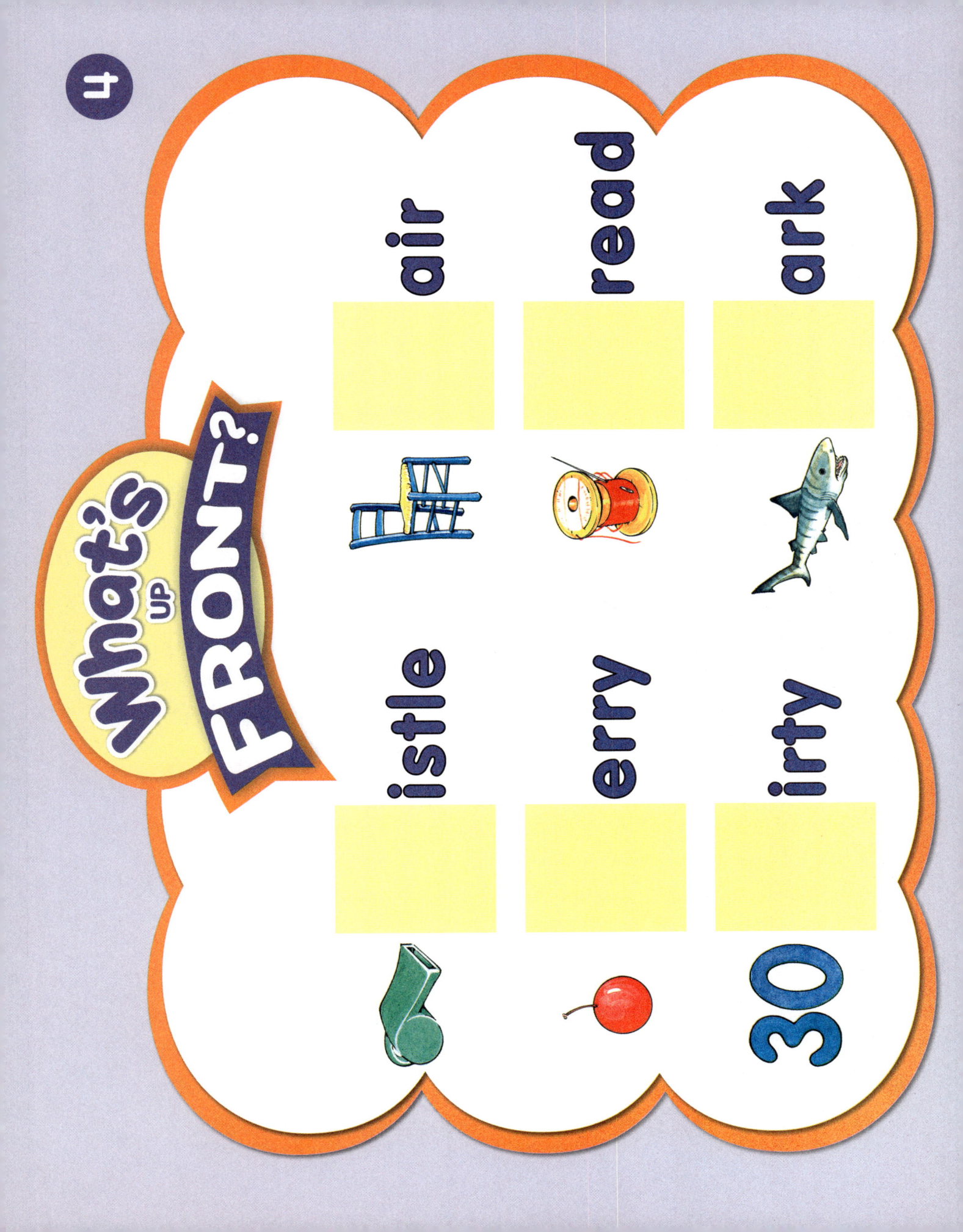

What's up FRONT?

air

read

ark

istle

erry

irty

30

Game 5

Phonics Games, Level C
EMC 3364 • © Evan-Moor Corp.

What's up FRONT?

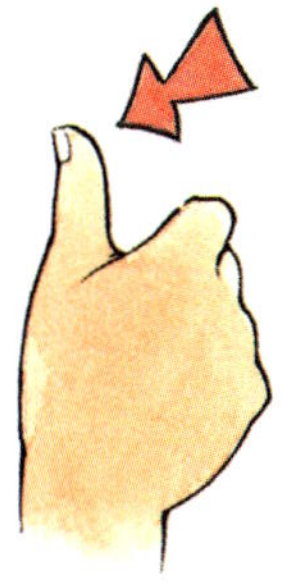

umb _____

ell _____

isper _____

irt _____

eel _____

eese _____

Game 5

Phonics Games, Level C
EMC 3364 • © Evan-Moor Corp.

What's UP FRONT?

ree

air

oe

3

eep

ale

ain

Game 5

sh	sh	sh	sh	sh	sh
sh	sh	sh	sh	sh	ch
ch	ch	ch	ch	ch	ch
ch	ch	ch	ch	wh	wh
wh	wh	wh	wh	wh	wh
wh	wh	th	th	th	th
th	th	th	th	th	th

Game 5

Phonics Games, Level C
EMC 3364
© Evan-Moor Corp.

Game 5

Phonics Games, Level C
EMC 3364
© Evan-Moor Corp.

Game 5

Phonics Games, Level C
EMC 3364
© Evan-Moor Corp.

Game 5

Phonics Games, Level C
EMC 3364
© Evan-Moor Corp.

Game 5

Phonics Games, Level C
EMC 3364
© Evan-Moor Corp.

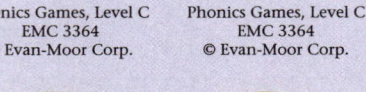

Game 5

Phonics Games, Level C
EMC 3364
© Evan-Moor Corp.

Game 5

Phonics Games, Level C
EMC 3364
© Evan-Moor Corp.

Game 5

Phonics Games, Level C
EMC 3364
© Evan-Moor Corp.

Game 5

Phonics Games, Level C
EMC 3364
© Evan-Moor Corp.

Game 5

Phonics Games, Level C
EMC 3364
© Evan-Moor Corp.

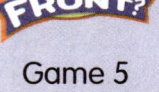

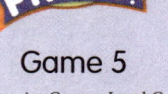

Game 5

Phonics Games, Level C
EMC 3364
© Evan-Moor Corp.

Game 5

Phonics Games, Level C
EMC 3364
© Evan-Moor Corp.

Game 5

Phonics Games, Level C
EMC 3364
© Evan-Moor Corp.

Game 5

Phonics Games, Level C
EMC 3364
© Evan-Moor Corp.

Game 5

Phonics Games, Level C
EMC 3364
© Evan-Moor Corp.

Game 5

Phonics Games, Level C
EMC 3364
© Evan-Moor Corp.

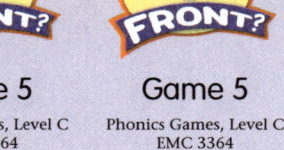

Game 5

Phonics Games, Level C
EMC 3364
© Evan-Moor Corp.

Game 5

Phonics Games, Level C
EMC 3364
© Evan-Moor Corp.

Game 5

Phonics Games, Level C
EMC 3364
© Evan-Moor Corp.

Game 5

Phonics Games, Level C
EMC 3364
© Evan-Moor Corp.

Game 5

Phonics Games, Level C
EMC 3364
© Evan-Moor Corp.

Game 5

Phonics Games, Level C
EMC 3364
© Evan-Moor Corp.

Game 5

Phonics Games, Level C
EMC 3364
© Evan-Moor Corp.

Game 5

Phonics Games, Level C
EMC 3364
© Evan-Moor Corp.

Game 5

Phonics Games, Level C
EMC 3364
© Evan-Moor Corp.

Game 5

Phonics Games, Level C
EMC 3364
© Evan-Moor Corp.

Game 5

Phonics Games, Level C
EMC 3364
© Evan-Moor Corp.

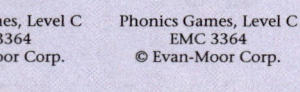

Game 5

Phonics Games, Level C
EMC 3364
© Evan-Moor Corp.

Game 5

Phonics Games, Level C
EMC 3364
© Evan-Moor Corp.

Game 5

Phonics Games, Level C
EMC 3364
© Evan-Moor Corp.

Game 5

Phonics Games, Level C
EMC 3364
© Evan-Moor Corp.

Game 5

Phonics Games, Level C
EMC 3364
© Evan-Moor Corp.

Game 5

Phonics Games, Level C
EMC 3364
© Evan-Moor Corp.

Game 5

Phonics Games, Level C
EMC 3364
© Evan-Moor Corp.

Game 5

Phonics Games, Level C
EMC 3364
© Evan-Moor Corp.

Game 5

Phonics Games, Level C
EMC 3364
© Evan-Moor Corp.

Game 5

Phonics Games, Level C
EMC 3364
© Evan-Moor Corp.

Game 5

Phonics Games, Level C
EMC 3364
© Evan-Moor Corp.

Game 5

Phonics Games, Level C
EMC 3364
© Evan-Moor Corp.

Game 5

Phonics Games, Level C
EMC 3364
© Evan-Moor Corp.

Game 5

Phonics Games, Level C
EMC 3364
© Evan-Moor Corp.

Spelling words with initial consonant digraphs

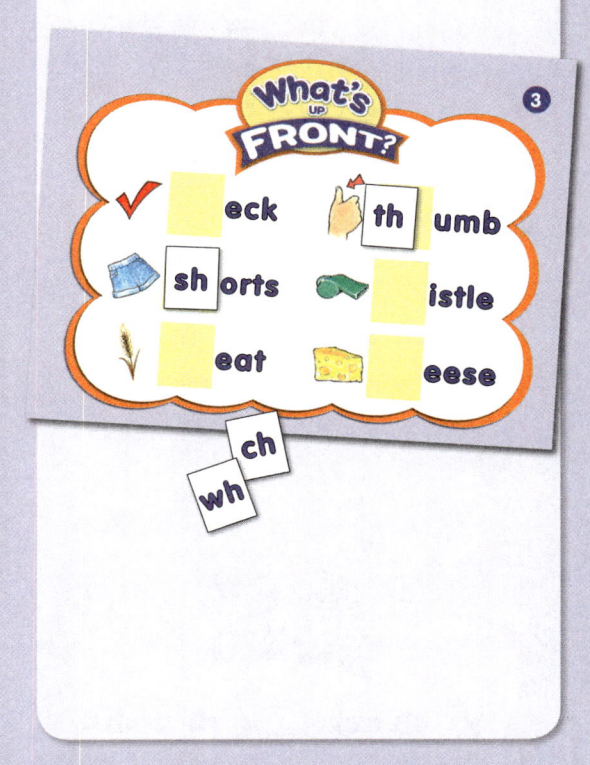

How to Check:

1. Each game board has a number.

2. Find your game board.

3. Look at the picture of your game board to check your answers.

1

What's UP FRONT?

ch ain · 30 th irty
wh eat · sh ell
sh irt · ✔ ch eck

2

What's UP FRONT?

sh oe · wh ale
wh eel · 3 th ree
ch erry · sh ark

3

What's UP FRONT?

✔ ch eck · th umb
sh orts · wh istle
wh eat · ch eese

4

What's UP FRONT?

wh istle · ch air
ch erry · th read
30 th irty · sh ark

5

What's UP FRONT?

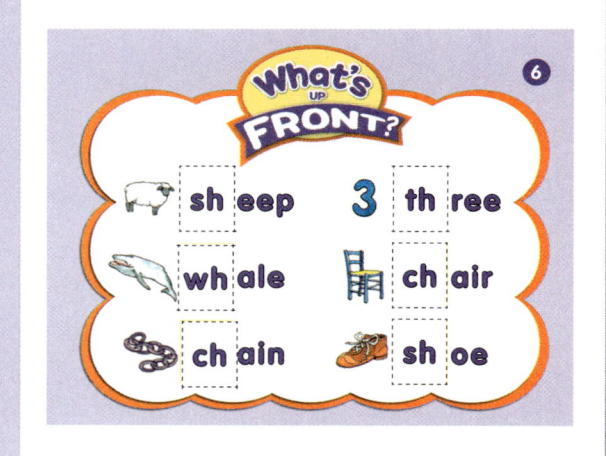

sh irt · th umb
wh eel · sh ell
ch eese · wh isper

6

What's UP FRONT?

sh eep · 3 th ree
wh ale · ch air
ch ain · sh oe

fold

Digraph Needed

Write the missing letters to spell each word.

| ch | sh | th | wh |

1. 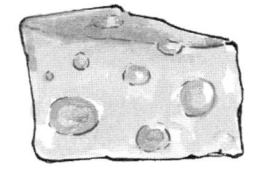 ___eese

2. 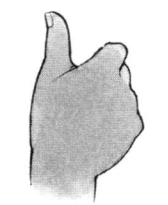 ___umb

3.  ___ell

4.  ___ick

5.  ___ale

6.  ___irty

Name _____

A Day at the Beach

Write letters to complete each word.

> th   wh   ch   sh

1. I like to find ___ells at the beach.

2. Dad often sleeps in the ___ade.

3. I ___row a ball to our dog.

4. The dog likes to ___ase the ball in the sand.

5. ___ile we play, Mom reads a book.

6. We never see ___arks or ___ales in the water.

7. I ___ink a day at the beach is great!

R-Controlled BINGO

*Reading words with **r**-controlled vowels*

Play

1. Place the **r**-controlled vowel cards faceup in a row in front of the caller.

2. The caller picks a word card from the bag. The caller reads the word aloud and does not show the card.

3. The players look for the word on their game boards. If they find the word, they cover it with a marker.

4. The caller places the word card below the correct **r**-controlled vowel card and picks another word card from the bag.

Win

1. A player must cover a row of words to win. The row can go up and down, across, or diagonally.

2. The first player to cover a row shouts out, "Bingo!"

3. The player reads the words aloud. The caller checks to make sure all of the words are below the vowel cards. If they are, the player wins!

Each player needs:

- 1 game board
- Markers (such as beans)

The caller needs:

- Vowel cards
- Word cards

Put the word cards into a bag.

Phonics Games, Level C • EMC 3364 • © Evan-Moor Corp.

R-Controlled BINGO 1

bird	water	burn	dirt	card
river	ladder	spark	fork	purple
farm	north	**FREE**	letter	chirp
over	yarn	girl	hurt	arm
nurse	stork	fern	star	winter

Game 6

Phonics Games, Level C
EMC 3364 • © Evan-Moor Corp.

R-Controlled BINGO 2

purple	horse	park	finger	dark
her	shirt	form	letter	turtle
born	surf	FREE	jar	stir
shark	third	horn	cart	purse
barn	over	swirl	river	curl

Game 6

Phonics Games, Level C
EMC 3364 • © Evan-Moor Corp.

R-Controlled BINGO 3

arm	form	winter	over	chirp
stork	card	burn	water	corn
ladder	fern	FREE	horn	yarn
her	forty	spark	curl	letter
north	purple	dirt	horse	first

Game 6

Phonics Games, Level C
EMC 3364 • © Evan-Moor Corp.

R-Controlled BINGO 4

cart	fork	swirl	nurse	first
burn	shirt	farm	river	hurt
park	corn	**FREE**	barn	turn
stir	dark	finger	north	star
girl	jar	born	third	purse

Game 6

Phonics Games, Level C
EMC 3364 • © Evan-Moor Corp.

R-Controlled BINGO 5

turn	her	dark	forty	third
winter	star	curl	nurse	first
stork	water	FREE	dirt	card
fern	river	jar	turtle	ladder
yarn	corn	farm	horn	chirp

Game 6

Phonics Games, Level C
EMC 3364 • © Evan-Moor Corp.

R-Controlled BINGO 6

shark	born	letter	purse	yarn
horse	cart	surf	bird	arm
shirt	hurt	FREE	forty	spark
form	third	barn	park	turn
turtle	stir	fork	burn	finger

Game 6

Phonics Games, Level C
EMC 3364 • © Evan-Moor Corp.

bird	stir	shirt	girl
first	dirt	third	swirl
chirp	her	river	finger
water	ladder	over	winter
fern	letter	surf	purple
curl	nurse	burn	purse

Game 6

Phonics Games, Level C
EMC 3364
© Evan-Moor Corp.

Game 6

Phonics Games, Level C
EMC 3364
© Evan-Moor Corp.

Game 6

Phonics Games, Level C
EMC 3364
© Evan-Moor Corp.

Game 6

Phonics Games, Level C
EMC 3364
© Evan-Moor Corp.

Game 6

Phonics Games, Level C
EMC 3364
© Evan-Moor Corp.

Game 6

Phonics Games, Level C
EMC 3364
© Evan-Moor Corp.

Game 6

Phonics Games, Level C
EMC 3364
© Evan-Moor Corp.

Game 6

Phonics Games, Level C
EMC 3364
© Evan-Moor Corp.

Game 6

Phonics Games, Level C
EMC 3364
© Evan-Moor Corp.

Game 6

Phonics Games, Level C
EMC 3364
© Evan-Moor Corp.

Game 6

Phonics Games, Level C
EMC 3364
© Evan-Moor Corp.

Game 6

Phonics Games, Level C
EMC 3364
© Evan-Moor Corp.

Game 6

Phonics Games, Level C
EMC 3364
© Evan-Moor Corp.

Game 6

Phonics Games, Level C
EMC 3364
© Evan-Moor Corp.

Game 6

Phonics Games, Level C
EMC 3364
© Evan-Moor Corp.

Game 6

Phonics Games, Level C
EMC 3364
© Evan-Moor Corp.

Game 6

Phonics Games, Level C
EMC 3364
© Evan-Moor Corp.

Game 6

Phonics Games, Level C
EMC 3364
© Evan-Moor Corp.

Game 6

Phonics Games, Level C
EMC 3364
© Evan-Moor Corp.

Game 6

Phonics Games, Level C
EMC 3364
© Evan-Moor Corp.

Game 6

Phonics Games, Level C
EMC 3364
© Evan-Moor Corp.

Game 6

Phonics Games, Level C
EMC 3364
© Evan-Moor Corp.

Game 6

Phonics Games, Level C
EMC 3364
© Evan-Moor Corp.

Game 6

Phonics Games, Level C
EMC 3364
© Evan-Moor Corp.

turn	turtle	hurt	cart
star	jar	arm	barn
card	yarn	park	dark
fork	horn	horse	corn
north	stork	forty	born
form	spark	farm	shark

Game 6

Phonics Games, Level C
EMC 3364
© Evan-Moor Corp.

Game 6

Phonics Games, Level C
EMC 3364
© Evan-Moor Corp.

Game 6

Phonics Games, Level C
EMC 3364
© Evan-Moor Corp.

Game 6

Phonics Games, Level C
EMC 3364
© Evan-Moor Corp.

Game 6

Phonics Games, Level C
EMC 3364
© Evan-Moor Corp.

Game 6

Phonics Games, Level C
EMC 3364
© Evan-Moor Corp.

Game 6

Phonics Games, Level C
EMC 3364
© Evan-Moor Corp.

Game 6

Phonics Games, Level C
EMC 3364
© Evan-Moor Corp.

Game 6

Phonics Games, Level C
EMC 3364
© Evan-Moor Corp.

Game 6

Phonics Games, Level C
EMC 3364
© Evan-Moor Corp.

Game 6

Phonics Games, Level C
EMC 3364
© Evan-Moor Corp.

Game 6

Phonics Games, Level C
EMC 3364
© Evan-Moor Corp.

Game 6

Phonics Games, Level C
EMC 3364
© Evan-Moor Corp.

Game 6

Phonics Games, Level C
EMC 3364
© Evan-Moor Corp.

Game 6

Phonics Games, Level C
EMC 3364
© Evan-Moor Corp.

Game 6

Phonics Games, Level C
EMC 3364
© Evan-Moor Corp.

Game 6

Phonics Games, Level C
EMC 3364
© Evan-Moor Corp.

Game 6

Phonics Games, Level C
EMC 3364
© Evan-Moor Corp.

Game 6

Phonics Games, Level C
EMC 3364
© Evan-Moor Corp.

Game 6

Phonics Games, Level C
EMC 3364
© Evan-Moor Corp.

Game 6

Phonics Games, Level C
EMC 3364
© Evan-Moor Corp.

Game 6

Phonics Games, Level C
EMC 3364
© Evan-Moor Corp.

Game 6

Phonics Games, Level C
EMC 3364
© Evan-Moor Corp.

Game 6

Phonics Games, Level C
EMC 3364
© Evan-Moor Corp.

ir

er

ar

ur

or

Game 6

Phonics Games, Level C
EMC 3364 • © Evan-Moor Corp.

Game 6

Phonics Games, Level C
EMC 3364 • © Evan-Moor Corp.

Game 6

Phonics Games, Level C
EMC 3364 • © Evan-Moor Corp.

Game 6

Phonics Games, Level C
EMC 3364 • © Evan-Moor Corp.

Game 6

Phonics Games, Level C
EMC 3364 • © Evan-Moor Corp.

Name _____

Meet Smarty

Read each sentence. Look at the underlined word or words.
Circle the letters that make the vowel + *r* sound.

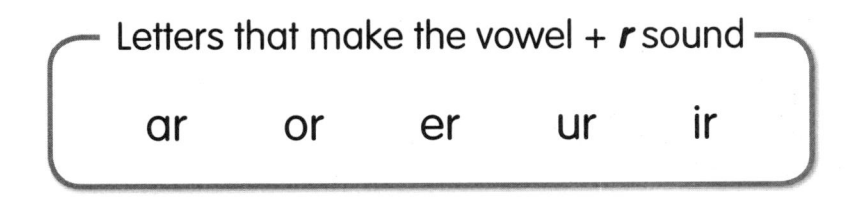

Letters that make the vowel + *r* sound

ar   or   er   ur   ir

1. The <u>barn</u> on our farm is red.

2. We have a <u>horse</u> named Smarty.

3. <u>Smarty</u> sleeps inside the barn at night.

4. Dad uses a big <u>fork</u> to stack hay.

5. Smarty chews hay and drinks <u>water</u>.

6. Smarty <u>lowers</u> his head to drink.

7. Smarty's body is <u>covered</u> in hair, not <u>fur</u>.

8. I keep each hoof free from <u>dirt</u>.

9. Smarty is my favorite animal on the <u>farm</u>.

Name _____

What Do You Hear?

Say each picture name.
Fill in the circle next to the sound you hear.

1.	○ er ○ ar ○ ur	2.	○ ir ○ or ○ ar
3.	○ or ○ er ○ ar	4.	○ ar ○ ir ○ ur
5.	○ ar ○ ir ○ or	6.	○ ir ○ er ○ or
7.	○ or ○ er ○ ar	8. 40	○ or ○ ir ○ ur
9.	○ ar ○ ur ○ or	10.	○ ar ○ ir ○ or

Phonics Games, Level C • EMC 3364 • © Evan-Moor Corp.

Syllable Count

Identifying 1-, 2-, and 3-syllable words

Play

1. Assign three players to each set.
2. The first player in each group picks a card from the bag and reads the word aloud.
3. The player determines the number of syllables in the word and places the card in a box next to 1, 2, or 3 on his or her game board. The next player takes a turn.
4. If a player picks a word card, counts the syllables, and determines that all of the boxes next to that number are already covered, the player puts the card back into the bag. The next player takes a turn.

Win

1. The first player to cover all six boxes on the game board shouts out, "I win!"
2. Players check the answer key to see if the cards are correctly placed.
3. If the player who shouted "I win!" has correctly placed the cards, he or she wins!

Set A players need:

- Game boards
- Cards
- Answer key
- Brown paper bag

Set B players need:

- Game boards
- Cards
- Answer key
- Brown paper bag

Game 7 • Set A

Phonics Games, Level C
EMC 3364 • © Evan-Moor Corp.

Game 7 • Set A

Phonics Games, Level C
EMC 3364 • © Evan-Moor Corp.

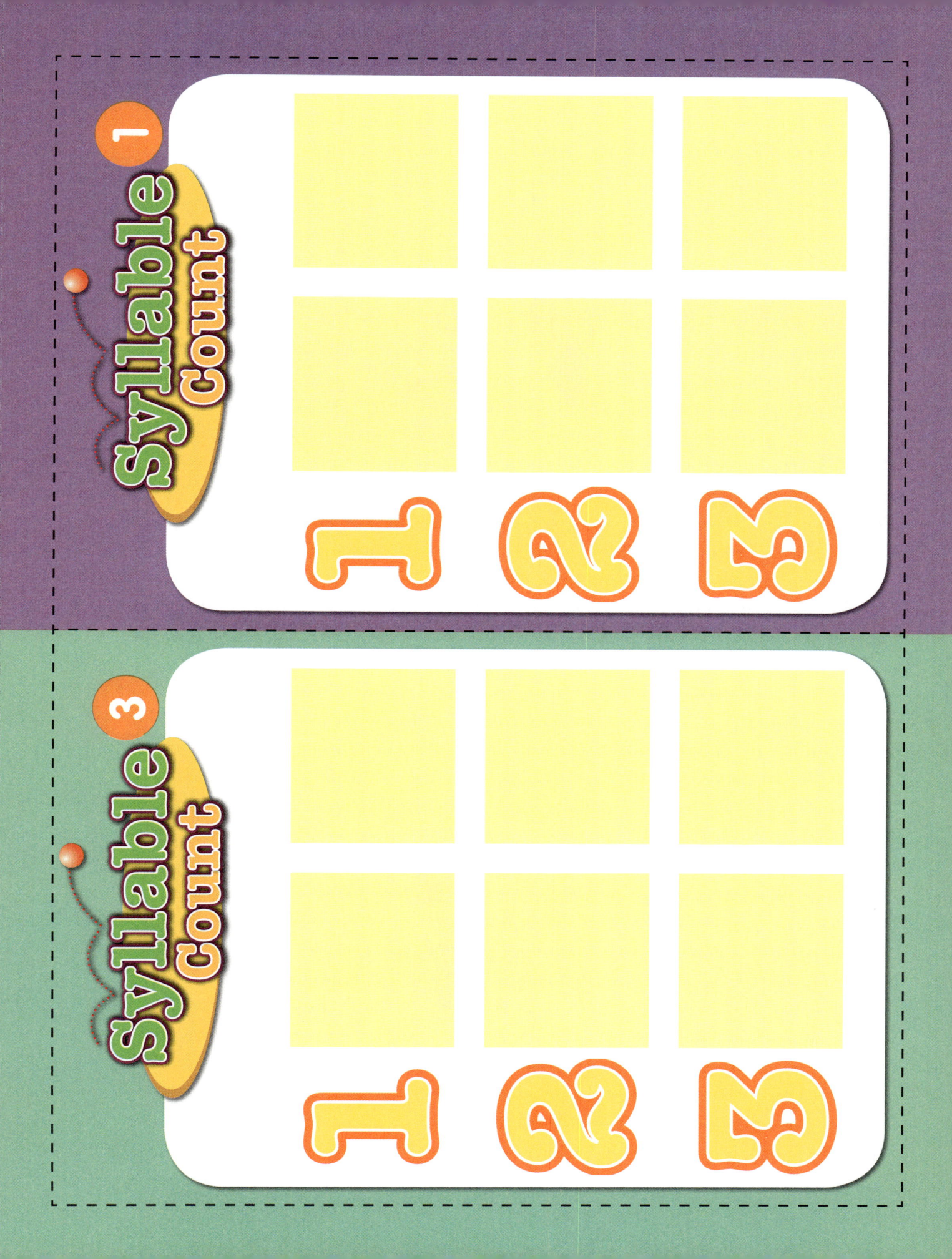

Syllable Count

Game 7 • Set B

Phonics Games, Level C
EMC 3364 • © Evan-Moor Corp.

Syllable Count

Game 7 • Set A

Phonics Games, Level C
EMC 3364 • © Evan-Moor Corp.

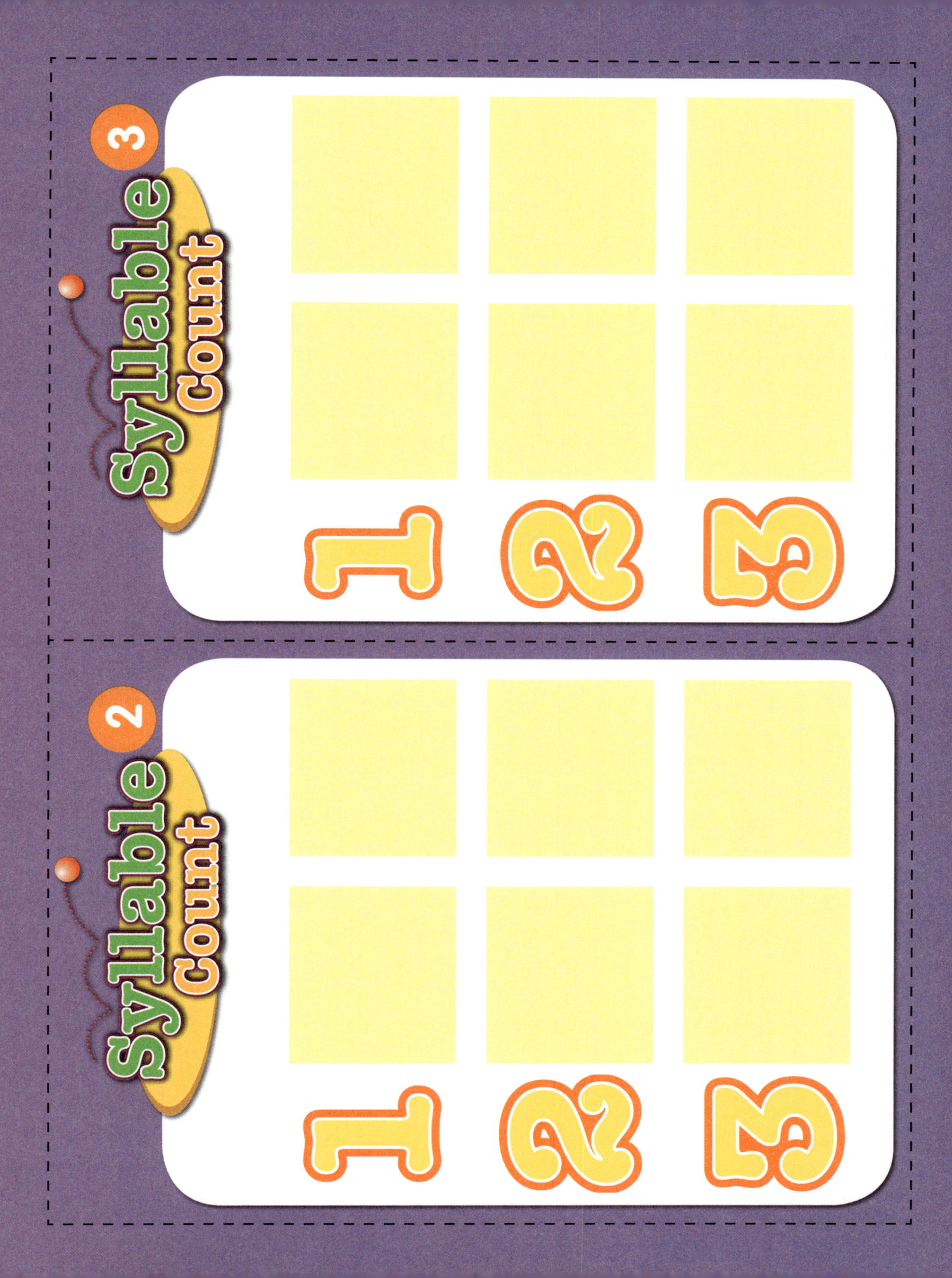

Syllable Count

Game 7 • Set B

Phonics Games, Level C
EMC 3364 • © Evan-Moor Corp.

Syllable Count

Game 7 • Set B

Phonics Games, Level C
EMC 3364 • © Evan-Moor Corp.

boot	clown	globe	goat
hand	leaf	pig	shoe
snake	apple	baby	balloon
cowboy	lion	monkey	feather
turtle	wagon	banana	butterfly
dinosaur	elephant	hamburger	pajamas
seventy	telephone	umbrella	

Game 7 • Set A
Phonics Games, Level C
EMC 3364
© Evan-Moor Corp.

Game 7 • Set A
Phonics Games, Level C
EMC 3364
© Evan-Moor Corp.

Game 7 • Set A
Phonics Games, Level C
EMC 3364
© Evan-Moor Corp.

Game 7 • Set A
Phonics Games, Level C
EMC 3364
© Evan-Moor Corp.

Game 7 • Set A
Phonics Games, Level C
EMC 3364
© Evan-Moor Corp.

Game 7 • Set A
Phonics Games, Level C
EMC 3364
© Evan-Moor Corp.

Game 7 • Set A
Phonics Games, Level C
EMC 3364
© Evan-Moor Corp.

Game 7 • Set A
Phonics Games, Level C
EMC 3364
© Evan-Moor Corp.

Game 7 • Set A
Phonics Games, Level C
EMC 3364
© Evan-Moor Corp.

Game 7 • Set A
Phonics Games, Level C
EMC 3364
© Evan-Moor Corp.

Game 7 • Set A
Phonics Games, Level C
EMC 3364
© Evan-Moor Corp.

Game 7 • Set A
Phonics Games, Level C
EMC 3364
© Evan-Moor Corp.

Game 7 • Set A
Phonics Games, Level C
EMC 3364
© Evan-Moor Corp.

Game 7 • Set A
Phonics Games, Level C
EMC 3364
© Evan-Moor Corp.

Game 7 • Set A
Phonics Games, Level C
EMC 3364
© Evan-Moor Corp.

Game 7 • Set A
Phonics Games, Level C
EMC 3364
© Evan-Moor Corp.

Game 7 • Set A
Phonics Games, Level C
EMC 3364
© Evan-Moor Corp.

Game 7 • Set A
Phonics Games, Level C
EMC 3364
© Evan-Moor Corp.

Game 7 • Set A
Phonics Games, Level C
EMC 3364
© Evan-Moor Corp.

Game 7 • Set A
Phonics Games, Level C
EMC 3364
© Evan-Moor Corp.

Game 7 • Set A
Phonics Games, Level C
EMC 3364
© Evan-Moor Corp.

Game 7 • Set A
Phonics Games, Level C
EMC 3364
© Evan-Moor Corp.

Game 7 • Set A
Phonics Games, Level C
EMC 3364
© Evan-Moor Corp.

Game 7 • Set A
Phonics Games, Level C
EMC 3364
© Evan-Moor Corp.

Game 7 • Set A
Phonics Games, Level C
EMC 3364
© Evan-Moor Corp.

Game 7 • Set A
Phonics Games, Level C
EMC 3364
© Evan-Moor Corp.

Game 7 • Set A
Phonics Games, Level C
EMC 3364
© Evan-Moor Corp.

pie	dish	dog	doll
frog	grapes	paint	pear
pink	basket	rainbow	flower
button	cherries	pencil	pizza
whistle	water	newspaper	bicycle
computer	gorilla	kangaroo	tomato
strawberry	octopus	skeleton	

Game 7 • Set B
Phonics Games, Level C
EMC 3364
© Evan-Moor Corp.

Game 7 • Set B
Phonics Games, Level C
EMC 3364
© Evan-Moor Corp.

Game 7 • Set B
Phonics Games, Level C
EMC 3364
© Evan-Moor Corp.

Game 7 • Set B
Phonics Games, Level C
EMC 3364
© Evan-Moor Corp.

Game 7 • Set B
Phonics Games, Level C
EMC 3364
© Evan-Moor Corp.

Game 7 • Set B
Phonics Games, Level C
EMC 3364
© Evan-Moor Corp.

Game 7 • Set B
Phonics Games, Level C
EMC 3364
© Evan-Moor Corp.

Game 7 • Set B
Phonics Games, Level C
EMC 3364
© Evan-Moor Corp.

Game 7 • Set B
Phonics Games, Level C
EMC 3364
© Evan-Moor Corp.

Game 7 • Set B
Phonics Games, Level C
EMC 3364
© Evan-Moor Corp.

Game 7 • Set B
Phonics Games, Level C
EMC 3364
© Evan-Moor Corp.

Game 7 • Set B
Phonics Games, Level C
EMC 3364
© Evan-Moor Corp.

Game 7 • Set B
Phonics Games, Level C
EMC 3364
© Evan-Moor Corp.

Game 7 • Set B
Phonics Games, Level C
EMC 3364
© Evan-Moor Corp.

Game 7 • Set B
Phonics Games, Level C
EMC 3364
© Evan-Moor Corp.

Game 7 • Set B
Phonics Games, Level C
EMC 3364
© Evan-Moor Corp.

Game 7 • Set B
Phonics Games, Level C
EMC 3364
© Evan-Moor Corp.

Game 7 • Set B
Phonics Games, Level C
EMC 3364
© Evan-Moor Corp.

Game 7 • Set B
Phonics Games, Level C
EMC 3364
© Evan-Moor Corp.

Game 7 • Set B
Phonics Games, Level C
EMC 3364
© Evan-Moor Corp.

Game 7 • Set B
Phonics Games, Level C
EMC 3364
© Evan-Moor Corp.

Game 7 • Set B
Phonics Games, Level C
EMC 3364
© Evan-Moor Corp.

Game 7 • Set B
Phonics Games, Level C
EMC 3364
© Evan-Moor Corp.

Game 7 • Set B
Phonics Games, Level C
EMC 3364
© Evan-Moor Corp.

Game 7 • Set B
Phonics Games, Level C
EMC 3364
© Evan-Moor Corp.

Game 7 • Set B
Phonics Games, Level C
EMC 3364
© Evan-Moor Corp.

Game 7 • Set B
Phonics Games, Level C
EMC 3364
© Evan-Moor Corp.

Set
A

Set
B

Answer Key

Answer Key

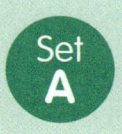

Syllable Count

Syllable Count

Identifying 1-, 2-, and 3-syllable words

Identifying 1-, 2-, and 3-syllable words

How to Check:

1. Look at the 1-syllable words under the number 1 on the answer key.

2. See if the words in the 1-syllable boxes on your game board are on the list.

3. If they are, you correctly placed the cards.

4. Check your 2- and 3-syllable words.

How to Check:

1. Look at the 1-syllable words under the number 1 on the answer key.

2. See if the words in the 1-syllable boxes on your game board are on the list.

3. If they are, you correctly placed the cards.

4. Check your 2- and 3-syllable words.

Count and Glue

Cut out each animal name.
Say the animal name and glue it below the number of syllables you hear.

1 Syllable	2 Syllables	3 Syllables
glue	glue	glue
glue	glue	glue
glue	glue	glue
glue	glue	glue

rabbit	kangaroo	monkey	horse
elephant	shark	zebra	goat
worm	tiger	octopus	butterfly

Name _____

How Many Syllables?

Read each word.
Circle the number that shows how many syllables you hear.

1. **bread** **1 2 3**	2. **orange** **1 2 3**	3. **apple** **1 2 3**
4. **hamburger** **1 2 3**	5. **rice** **1 2 3**	6. **potato** **1 2 3**
7. **plum** **1 2 3**	8. **strawberry** **1 2 3**	9. **cheese** **1 2 3**
10. **carrot** **1 2 3**	11. **banana** **1 2 3**	12. **cookie** **1 2 3**

Phonics Games Answer Key

LEVEL C

Page 25—What's That Sound?

blend – short e   chase – long a
boss – short o   huge – long u
clap – short a   sleep – long e
jump – short u   bone – long o
fin – short i   fine – long i

Page 26—Color the Blanket

Color	Word
red	desk, blend, rest
blue	tube, mule, blue
green	reach, week, feet
yellow	hole, joke, bone

Page 39—Sorting Sounds

long a – pail, tray
long e – deal, jeep
long i – bite, night
long o – moan, crow
long u – glue, tool, fruit, spool

Page 40—Vowel Digraphs

1. oo   4. oa   7. ea
2. igh   5. ea   8. ee
3. ue   6. oo   9. ui

Page 59—It Begins With…

1. fl   4. tr   7. cl
2. sw   5. gl   8. sk
3. st   6. sm   9. gr

Page 60—Hear the Blend

1. cr   5. tr
2. gl   6. gl
3. sl   7. sp
4. br   8. st

Page 81—Long Vowel Sounds

1. rail, stay, page
2. pool, glue, juice
3. bike, might, pies
4. know, vote, goat
5. clean, teeth, we

Page 82—About Moose

a – lakes, wade
e – eat, very, trees, deep
i – like, high
o – grow, snow
u – Moose, blue

Page 101—Digraph Needed

1. ch   4. ch
2. th   5. wh
3. sh   6. th

Page 102—A Day at the Beach

1. sh   5. Wh
2. sh   6. sh, wh
3. th   7. th
4. ch

Page 123—Meet Smarty

1. barn   6. lowers
2. horse   7. covered, fur
3. Smarty   8. dirt
4. fork   9. farm
5. water

Page 124—What Do You Hear?

1. ar   6. or
2. ir   7. ar
3. er   8. or
4. ur   9. ur
5. ar   10. ar

Page 139—Count and Glue

1 Syllable	2 Syllables	3 Syllables
goat	monkey	butterfly
horse	rabbit	elephant
shark	tiger	kangaroo
worm	zebra	octopus

Page 140—How Many Syllables?

1. 1 syllable   7. 1 syllable
2. 2 syllables   8. 3 syllables
3. 2 syllables   9. 1 syllable
4. 3 syllables   10. 2 syllables
5. 1 syllable   11. 3 syllables
6. 3 syllables   12. 2 syllables

Word Family Fun—from Start to Finish!

Start with engaging stories and activities; finish with fun-to-play games.

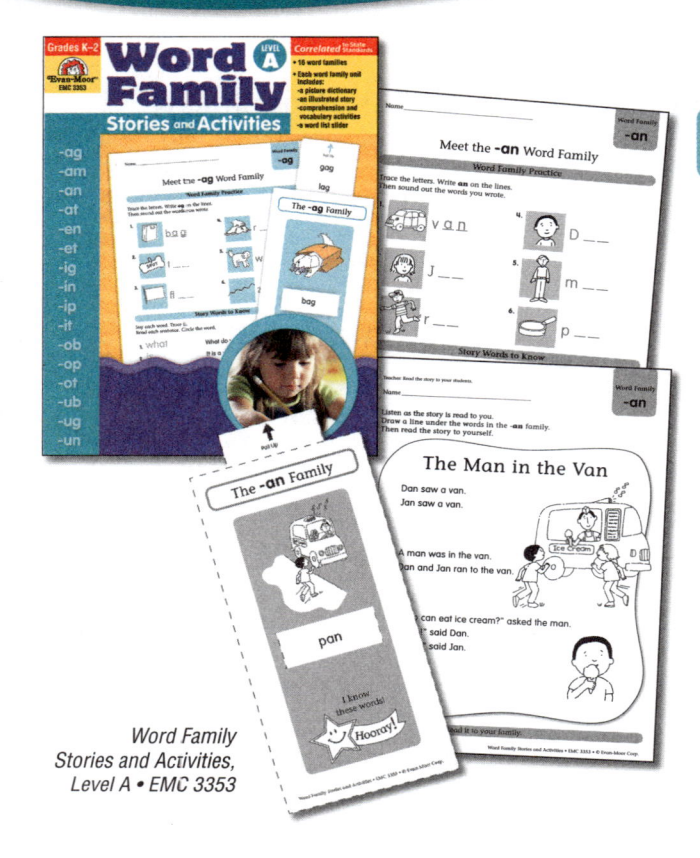

Word Family Stories and Activities, Level A • EMC 3353

Word Family Stories and Activities

Each *Word Family Stories and Activities* book contains practice for 16 word families. You get a 5-page reproducible unit for each word family containing: a picture dictionary to introduce the words, an engaging one-page story, comprehension and vocabulary activities, and a word list slider to practice reading for fluency. 112 pages. **Correlated to state standards.**

Word Family Stories and Activities, Level A
Practices these 16 CVC word families: -ag, -am, -an, -at, -en, -et, -ig, -in, -ip, -it, -ob, -op, -ot, -ub, -ug, and -un.

Grades K–2   EMC 3353

Word Family Stories and Activities, Level B
Practices these 16 short vowel word families: -ack, -and, -atch, -ell, -ent, -est, -ick, -ill, -ing, -ink, -ock, -og, -um, -ung, -unk, and -ush.

Grades K–2   EMC 3354

Word Family Stories and Activities, Level C
Practices these 16 long vowel word families: -ail, -ake, -ame, -ate, -ay, -eat, -ee, -eep, -eeze, -ice, -ide, -ine, -oke, -old, -ow, and -y.

Grades 1–3   EMC 3355

Word Family Stories and Activities, Level D
Practices these 16 word families: -ain, -are, -aw, -each, -ead, -ear, -ew, -ight, -itch, -ook, -ool, -ore, -ound, -own, -udge, and -ue.

Grades 1–3   EMC 3356

Word Family Games: Centers for Up to 6 Players Level A • EMC 3357

Word Family Games: Centers for Up to 6 Players

Word Family Games: Centers for Up to 6 Players provides fun, hands-on practice to increase word recognition and vocabulary skills. Each book contains 7 full-color games with materials for six players and a leader, plus two reproducible activity pages for extra word family practice. Word families practiced correspond to those presented in *Word Family Stories and Activities*. Students will eagerly practice word family words while trying to be the first to call "Bingo!" or "Four in a Row!" 144 full-color pages. **Correlated to state standards.**

Word Family Games, Level A
Grades K–2   EMC 3357

Word Family Games, Level B
Grades K–2   EMC 3358

Word Family Games, Level C
Grades 1–3   EMC 3359

Word Family Games, Level D
Grades 1–3   EMC 3360

High-Frequency Word Fun—from Start to Finish!

High-Frequency Words: Stories and Activities

Help students master the words that comprise nearly 50% of everything in print. *High-Frequency Words: Stories and Activities* contains everything young readers need for practice of high-frequency words. The 15 teaching units in each book help build fluency, automaticity, and comprehension with engaging reproducible one-page activities, stories, and word-list sliders. There are also pretests, cumulative word lists to use as assessments, and a certificate of achievement. Taken together, the four books cover the 220-word Dolch Basic Sight Vocabulary, as well as words from Fry's Instant Words lists. 112 full-color pages.

Correlated to state standards.

High-Frequency Words:
Stories and Activities, Level A
Grades K–1   EMC 3376

High-Frequency Words:
Stories and Activities, Level B
Grades K–1   EMC 3377

High-Frequency Words:
Stories and Activities, Level C
Grades 2–3   EMC 3378

High-Frequency Words:
Stories and Activities, Level D
Grades 2–3   EMC 3379

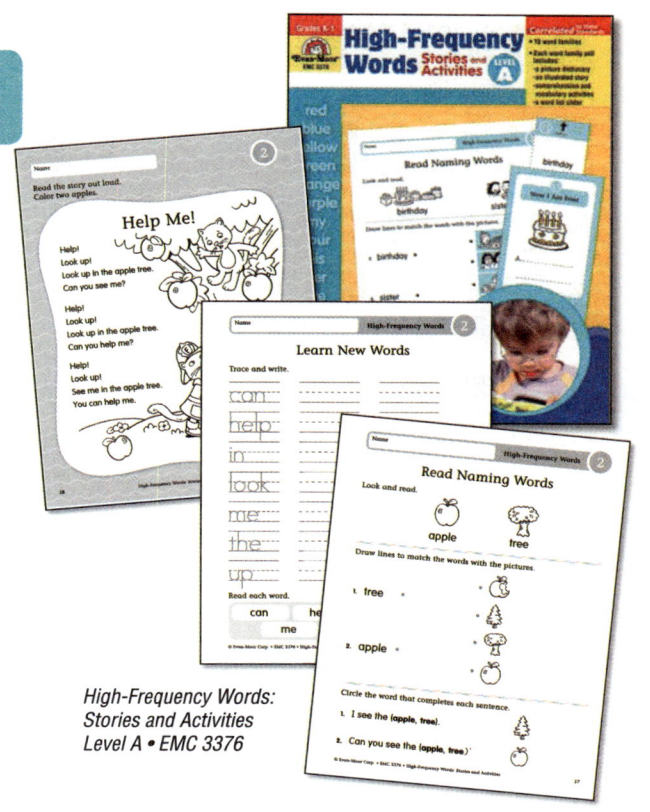

High-Frequency Words:
Stories and Activities
Level A • EMC 3376

High-Frequency Words: Center Games

High-Frequency Words: Center Games contains colorful and engaging game formats that provide students with the motivation they need to practice reading high-frequency words. Each of the four books provides practice based on Dolch Basic Sight Vocabulary, as well as words from Fry's Instant Words lists. Games such as Bingo, Concentration, and Ping, Pang, Pow! make high-frequency word recognition practice fun! 144 full-color pages.

Correlated to state standards.

High-Frequency Words:
Center Games, Level A
Grades K–1   EMC 3380

High-Frequency Words:
Center Games, Level B
Grades K–1   EMC 3381

High-Frequency Words:
Center Games, Level C
Grades 2–3   EMC 3382

High-Frequency Words:
Center Games, Level D
Grades 2–3   EMC 3383

High-Frequency Words:
Center Games
Level A • EMC 3380

Vocabulary Centers

The activities in *Vocabulary Centers* help build a rich vocabulary. The 12 full-color centers in each book contain task cards, games, and activity sheets. 192 full-color pages. **Correlated to state standards.**

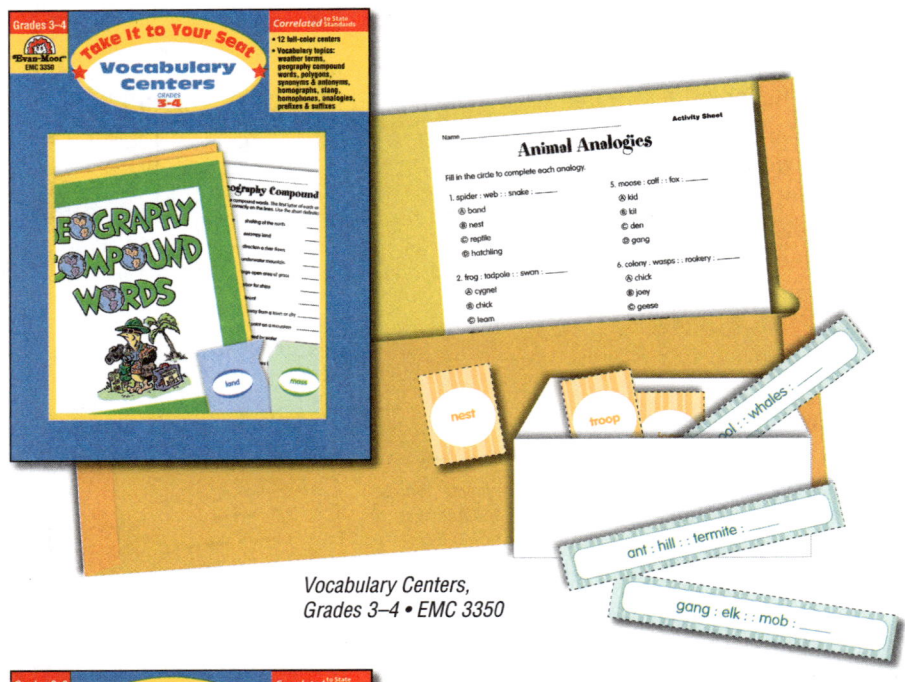

Vocabulary Centers,
Grades 3–4 • EMC 3350

Vocabulary Centers,
Grades 2–3 • EMC 3349

Vocabulary Centers, Grades K–1
Recognizing color words, identifying rhymes, reading sight words, categorizing, and more.
Grades K–1   EMC 3347

Vocabulary Centers, Grades 1–2
Categorizing nouns and animal groups, forming compounds, recognizing opposites, naming synonyms, and more.
Grades 1–2   EMC 3348

Vocabulary Centers, Grades 2–3
Making analogies, naming polygons, differentiating multiple meanings, describing feelings, and more.
Grades 2–3   EMC 3349

Vocabulary Centers, Grades 3–4
Differentiating homophones, using prefixes and suffixes, naming polygons, and more.
Grades 3–4   EMC 3350

Vocabulary Centers, Grades 4–5
Pronouncing heteronyms, recognizing science content words, naming geometric figures, recognizing music terms, and more.
Grades 4–5   EMC 3351

Vocabulary Centers, Grades 5–6
Recognizing acronyms, creating analogies, recognizing biomes, differentiating homographs, and more.
Grades 5–6   *EMC 3352*